Get the Signal!

Discourse Markers for Reading and Writing

Tatsuki Sato
Shunsuke Uchino

Ayed Hasian

JN084376

KINSEIDO

Kinseido Publishing Co., Ltd.

3-21 Kanda Jimbo-cho, Chiyoda-ku,
Tokyo 101-0051, Japan

First published 2023 by Kinseido Publishing Co., Ltd.

Cover design: Takayuki Minegishi
Text design: Asahi Media International Inc.
Illustrations: Toru Igarashi

🎧 音声ファイル無料ダウンロード

https://www.kinsei-do.co.jp/download/4181

**この教科書で 🎧 DL 00 の表示がある箇所の音声は、上記 URL または QR コードにて
無料でダウンロードできます。自習用音声としてご活用ください。**

 ▶ PC からのダウンロードをお勧めします。スマートフォンなどでダウンロードされる場合は、
  ダウンロード前に「解凍アプリ」をインストールしてください。
 ▶ URL は、**検索ボックスではなくアドレスバー（URL 表示欄）** に入力してください。
 ▶ お使いのネットワーク環境によっては、ダウンロードできない場合があります。

 ◎ **CD 00** 左記の表示がある箇所の音声は、教室用 CD（Class Audio CD）に収録されています。

はじめに

　本テキストでは、ディスコースマーカーの理解や活用を軸として、リーディング・ライティング活動を中心に、英語力を総合的に育成することを目指します。ディスコースマーカーとは、文章や発言の意図を理解しやすくする「つなぎ言葉」です。例えば、次の文を見てください。（　　　）の中には、どのような言葉を入れますか。

　出席番号順に弁当を受け取ることになった。（　　　）、最初に弁当を手に取ったのは渡辺くんだった。

　多くの人は、「でも」や「だけど」、「しかし」などの言葉を入れるでしょう。では、「だから」や「それで」という言葉は入るでしょうか。日本の多くの学校では出席番号は名前のアイウエオ順ですが、一部の学校では誕生日によって出席番号が決まります。上の文がそのような学校の場面で、そして「渡辺くん」が4月2日生まれの出席番号1番の生徒ならば、「でも」という言葉はむしろ不自然です。つまり、（　　　）の中に入る言葉によって、私たちは「渡辺くん」の出席番号が1番かどうかという、直接書かれていない情報を読み取ることができます。
　もう1つ、例を見てみましょう。

　バラ科の果物に対してアレルギーがあるので、実桜は食べられません。

　「実桜」が何か、皆さんは知っていますか。知らなくても、「実桜」がバラ科の果物であることは予想できます。一方で、次の文ではどうでしょうか。

　バラ科の果物に対してアレルギーがあります。あと、荔枝は食べられません。

　「荔枝」が何か分かる人は、多くはないでしょう。しかし、少なくとも、「荔枝」がバラ科の果物ではないことは予想できます。このように、「（な）ので」と「あと」という、異なるディスコースマーカーの力を借りて、その後の言葉がどのような言葉なのか、私たちは予想しやすくなります（ちなみに、「実桜」はサクランボで、「荔枝」はライチです）。
　ディスコースマーカーによって、直接書かれていない内容を理解しやすく、また、書かれていてもよく分からない内容を推測しやすくなります。本テキストを通して、ある程度の長さのある文章を読む楽しみや、自分が書いた英語が相手に伝わる喜びを、より多くの人が味わえることを期待しています。
　最後に、本テキストの完成に尽力してくださった金星堂編集部の皆様に、この場をお借りりして感謝申し上げます。
　——ところで、この「はじめに」には、いくつのディスコースマーカーが含まれているでしょうか。時間があれば数えてみてください。

著者一同

本テキストの使い方

本テキストの各Unitは、6ページで構成されています。Unitの前半ではリーディング、後半ではライティングの活動に取り組みます。また、音声がダウンロードできますので、リスニング・スピーキングの力を含め、英語力を総合的に伸ばせるよう、積極的に活用しましょう。

● Important Expressions（Unitの1ページ目・前半）

Unitの **Today's Article** に出てくる単語を確認します。提示されているアルファベットをヒントに、英単語を復元しましょう。音声には、日本語文に対応する英文が収録されていますので、予習や授業では、先生の指示に応じて使用しましょう。復習では、音声を聞いて英文全体を復元するディクテーションや、和文英訳の答え合わせなどに活用しましょう。

● Signal Check（Unitの1ページ目・後半）

Unitのテーマとなるディスコースマーカーを確認します。日本語に対応する英語のディスコースマーカーを確認し、この後に読む文章でどこに注目すればよいかを把握しましょう。

● Today's Article（Unitの2ページ目）

リーディング活動のメインとなる文章が掲載されています。Unitによって、ブログ、ネットの記事、SNSなど、さまざまな形式の文章を読むことができます。**Important Expressions** や **Signal Check** で確認した単語や表現に注意しながら読んでみましょう。文章の音声を聞くことができるので、予習や授業では、先生の指示に応じて使用しましょう。復習では、音読やシャドーイングなど、英語を定着させるために必要不可欠な活動を行いましょう。

● Take in the Article（Unitの3ページ目）

文章の内容をより深く理解するための演習問題です。**A**は、文章全体の概要を表の形式で整理する問題です。**B**と**C**では、文章の内容に関するTF問題とQA問題に取り組みます。それぞれ、問3では、皆さんが自分で問題を作成します。自分の英語力をフル活用して、オリジナルの問題を作ってみましょう。

● Focus on the Signal（Unitの4ページ目・前半）

Signal Check や **Today's Article** に登場したディスコースマーカーや、関連する表現を学習します。既に意味を知っている表現であっても、使い方を間違いやすいものがあります。特に、日本語と英語で使い方が異なる表現には注意しましょう。

● Use the Signal（Unitの4ページ目・後半）

Focus on the Signal で取り上げたディスコースマーカーの使い方を練習するための演

習問題です。**A**では、ディスコースマーカーの前後などをつなげる問題に、**B**では、ディスコースマーカーを用いた和文英訳問題に取り組みます。

● **Opinions on the Article**（Unit の 5 ページ目）

Express Your Opinions で取り組むライティング活動の準備をするための問題です。**Today's Article** の内容に対する、2 人の意見文が掲載されています。**A**は、英語で書かれた意見文を読み、内容を日本語で表に整理する問題です。**B**は、日本語で書かれた表の内容に基づいて、英語の意見文を完成させる穴埋め問題です。**A**と**B**の意見文は、賛成派と反対派など、異なる立場からの意見文になっています。問題に取り組みながら、**Express Your Opinions** のライティング活動で使えそうな表現をチェックしましょう。それぞれの英文には、音声がついています。**Today's Article** と同様に、音読やシャドーイングなど、英語を定着させるための活動に使用することができます。また、**Express Your Opinions** の内容を口頭で発表する場合にも、参考にしてみましょう。

● **Express Your Opinions**（Unit の 6 ページ目）

各 Unit の最後となるページでは、ライティングのメインとなる活動に取り組みます。**Today's Article** の内容に関して、意見文などのまとまりのある文章を書くことを目指します。まず、**A**で書きたい内容を日本語で表に整理しましょう。次に、**B**でその内容を英語で表現しましょう。**Opinions on the Article** の内容や表現をヒントにすることをお勧めします。また、ディスコースマーカーを用いて、内容をより分かりやすく伝える工夫をしてみましょう。最後に**C**で、**Opinions on the Article** の音声も参考にしながら、ライティングした内容を口頭で発表しましょう。

Contents

Good memory or good picture?

記憶に残すか、記録に残すか

反対の内容を伝える表現（1）**[but]**

Important Expressions

🎧 DL 02　💿 CD 02

[　　]内のアルファベットを並び替えて、下線部の日本語を表す英単語を完成させましょう。

1. 私は**ついこの間**、兄と動物園に行きました。　　　　　[c e e l n t y]（r _ _ _ _ _ _ _）

2. 君が**どこへ**行っ**ても**、私は君と一緒にいます。　　　[e e e h r r v]（w _ _ _ _ _ _ _）

3. ニュージーランドでのスカイダイビングは、私が決して忘れない**経験**です。

[c e e e i n p r x]（e _ _ _ _ _ _ _ _ _）

4. これをSNSに**投稿して**もいいですか。　　　　　　　　　　[o s t]（p _ _ _）

5. **個人的には**、彼は間違っていないと思います。　[a e l l n o r s y]（p _ _ _ _ _ _ _ _）

Signal Check

□　で囲まれている日本語に対応する英語に〇をつけましょう。

1. I don't play baseball, but I like watching it.

私は野球はしません　**が**、見るのは好きです。

2. "I overslept this morning." "But you weren't late for class."

「私は今朝、寝坊をしました」「　**でも**、授業に遅れませんでしたね」

3. I ate not only *ramen* but also fried rice for lunch.

私は昼食にラーメン　**だけでなく**、チャーハン　**も**食べました。

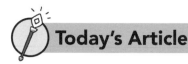 **Today's Article**

🎧 DL 03　💿 CD 03

次のブログを読みましょう。

 反対の意味を表す語に注意しながら読もう！

Picture crazy?

April 10, 2023 at 9:00 p.m.

I recently went to lunch with my daughter, Lana, and I noticed something interesting. Lana takes pictures of everything! Wherever we went, when
5　she saw something she liked, she took out her phone and snapped a picture. She does take really good pictures, but is a picture always necessary?

It was raining a little yesterday, but the rain stopped when we left the train station. At that moment, we noticed a rainbow in the sky. It was not just a normal rainbow, but a double rainbow! How lucky! I was happy to share
10　this experience with my daughter. She also looked happy and immediately took out her phone to take pictures. Double rainbows are rare, so I think she wanted to show other people, too.

After that, we went to a popular Italian restaurant. When our food arrived, I picked up my fork to start eating, but she picked up her phone again. This
15　time, she not only took a picture of her food, but also posted the picture online! I can understand taking a picture of a rainbow, but who wants to see pictures of food?

If she's happy, I'm happy, but am I the only one who thinks that's strange? Is she taking these pictures to show other people or to save the memory for
20　herself? Personally, I like to enjoy the moment. Pictures can't tell you how you felt at that time or how good food tastes. I guess this generation just enjoys things in a different way.

Notes

take out ~「～を取り出す」
snap「(写真を) 撮る」
at that moment「その時」
pick up ~「～を手に取る」
generation「世代」

Take in the Article

A Today's Articleの内容と合うように、空所に適切な日本語を書き入れましょう。

	筆者	ラナ
虹を見たとき	そのことを (¹.　　　) と共有した	(².　　　　　　) を取り出した
食事が来たとき	(³.　　　　　　　　) を手に取った	(⁴.　　　　　　) を手に取った

B Today's Articleの内容と合っていればT、そうでなければFを選びましょう。また、問3では、Today's Articleの内容に関するTF問題を英語で作り、ペアで問題を出しあいましょう。

1. The writer likes taking pictures more than her daughter.　　　　　[T / F]

2. The writer and her daughter seem to enjoy things in a different way.　　[T / F]

3. _____　[T / F]

C Today's Articleの内容と合うように、次の質問に英語で答えましょう。また、問3では、Today's Articleの内容に関する質問とその答えを英語で作り、ペアで問題を出しあいましょう。

1. Q Did the writer and her daughter see a normal rainbow?

A _____

2. Q What did Lana do after she took a picture of her food?

A _____

3. Q _____

A _____

Focus on the Signal

「(だ) けど」「(だ) が」「しかし」など、前の文と反対のことや、前の文からは予想しにくいことを続けて言いたいときは、**but** を使うことができます。

① I like coffee, **but** I don't like tea.
「私はコーヒーは好き**だけど**、紅茶は好きではありません」

but は②のように、前の文にカンマでつなげて使うことができます。③のように文の最初に **But** をつけるのは、会話文などのカジュアルな場面に限定されます。ライティングでは、文頭で **But** を用いるのは適切ではありません。日本語の「しかし」とは使い方が少し違うため、注意しましょう。

② ○ My father plays baseball well, **but** I play it better.
③ △ My father plays baseball well. **But** I play it better.
「私の父は野球がうまいです**が**、私の方がうまいです」

but を用いた、よく使われる表現も確認しましょう。

・**not ~ but** ... 「～ではなくて…」

④ This letter is **not** yours **but** mine.
「この手紙はあなたのもの**ではなく**私のものです」

・**not only ~ but also** ... 「～だけでなく…も」

⑤ He ate **not only** chicken **but also** fish.
「彼は鶏**だけ**でなく魚**も**食べました」

Use the Signal

A 空所に入る表現を a ~ c から選びましょう。

1. I like English songs, but (　　　). 　　a. I haven't practiced recently
2. I have 11 dogs, but (　　). 　　b. I want more
3. I belonged to a tennis club, but 　　c. I can't catch what they say
(　　).

B (　　) 内の語句をヒントにして、次の日本語を英語で表現しましょう。

1. 私は英語を勉強しましたが、他の言語は勉強していません。
(other languages)

_____

2. 私は漫画だけではなく小説も買いました。
(a comic book / a novel)

_____

Opinions on the Article

A ブログに対するトムのコメントに合うように、下の表の空所を埋めましょう。

 DL 04　CD 04

 I understand the writer's feelings. When we are with somebody, we should share as much time and as many experiences as possible. I sometimes take pictures of something beautiful when I'm out with my friends, but I won't post them online while I'm with them. This is because I prefer to talk with the people in front of me rather than somebody on the other side of the screen.

誰に共感するコメントか	(1.　　　　　　)
具体的なエピソード	友人と一緒にいるとき、(2.　　　　　　　　) ことはあるが (3.　　　　　　　　) はしない
理由	(4.　　　　　　　　) にいる人よりも (5.　　　　　　) にいる人と話がしたいから

B 表の内容と合うように、ブログに対するミオのコメントの空所に入る語を選択肢から選びましょう。

DL 05　CD 05

誰に共感するコメントか	ラナ
具体的なエピソード	きれいなものや面白いものの写真を毎日SNSに投稿し、友人と共有する
理由	対面だけでなくオンラインでのコミュニケーションも関係を良好に保つ上で重要であり、SNSへの投稿は自分自身を表現するための最も簡単な方法のひとつだと思うから

I understand (1.　　　　　　) feelings. I (2.　　　　　　) pictures of beautiful and funny things on social media to (3.　　　　　　) with my friends every day. I think that not only face-to-face but also online communication is important for good (4.　　　　　　). Posting on social media is one of the easiest ways to express (5.　　　　　　).

Lana's　　myself　　post　　relationships　　share

Express Your Opinions

何でも写真に撮ることの是非について、ブログへのコメントを書きましょう。

A 前ページの表にならい、意見をまとめましょう。

誰に共感するコメントか	
具体的なエピソード	
理由	

B 前ページのコメントにならい、上の表にまとめた内容を英語で書きましょう。

I understand (　　　　　　　　　　) feelings. ＿＿＿＿＿＿＿
＿＿＿＿＿＿＿＿＿＿＿＿＿＿＿＿＿＿＿＿＿＿＿＿＿＿
＿＿＿＿＿＿＿＿＿＿＿＿＿＿＿＿＿＿＿＿＿＿＿＿＿＿
＿＿＿＿＿＿＿＿＿＿＿＿＿＿＿＿＿＿＿＿＿＿＿＿＿＿
＿＿＿＿＿＿＿＿＿＿＿＿＿＿＿＿＿＿＿＿＿＿＿＿＿＿
＿＿＿＿＿＿＿＿＿＿＿＿＿＿＿＿＿＿＿＿＿＿＿＿＿＿
＿＿＿＿＿＿＿＿＿＿＿＿＿＿＿＿＿＿＿＿＿＿＿＿＿＿

✔ 使用した表現があればチェックをしましょう。

☐ but
☐ not ~ but ...
☐ not only ~ but also ...

C ペアやグループで発表しましょう。

UNIT 2

See you at Kasumigaseki Station!

日本旅行で気を付けること

 反対の内容を伝える表現（2） **[however]**

 Important Expressions

🎧 DL 06　◎ CD 06

[　]内のアルファベットを並び替えて、下線部の日本語を表す英単語を完成させましょう。

1. 前もって計画しておく必要があります。　　　　　　　　　[a d e h]（a ＿ ＿ ＿ ＿ ）

2. ここから名古屋駅までの停留所は３つです。　　　　　　　[o p t]（s ＿ ＿ ＿ ）

3. 自分でネイルを塗るのは面倒です。　　　　　　　　[b e l o r u]（t ＿ ＿ ＿ ＿ ＿ ＿ ）

4. 「了解しました」と、返事をしました。　　　　　　　　[e l p y]（r ＿ ＿ ＿ ＿ ）

5. 私たちはそのニュースに困惑しました。　　　　　[d e f n o s u]（c ＿ ＿ ＿ ＿ ＿ ＿ ＿ ）

 Signal Check

☐で囲まれている日本語に対応する英語に○をつけましょう。

1. She is my favorite singer. However, I don't like her new song.

彼女は私の大好きな歌手です。しかし、新曲は好きではありません。

2. I prepared handmade chocolate. On that day, however, he was absent.

私は手作りチョコを用意しました。しかし、彼はその日、休みでした。

3. I don't like horror movies. Yet, I enjoy haunted houses.

私はホラー映画が苦手です。でも、お化け屋敷には入れます。

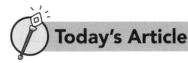

Today's Article

次の記事を読みましょう。

 but 以外の、反対の意味を表す語に注意しながら読もう！

 By Mark Taylor
May 15, 2023 at 3:00 p.m.

When I travel, I am usually very careful. I plan ahead, ask questions, and bring everything I think I might need. However, my first trip to Japan taught me that nobody is perfect.

After four great days with some friends in Osaka, I spent the next three days sightseeing in Kawagoe, Saitama. Before I left Japan, my friend Daisuke, who lives in Tokyo, said he wanted to pick me up at Kasumigaseki Station and see me off at the airport. He said it was the easiest place to meet because it was *jibun ni chikai*, which I learned in Osaka means "close to you."

Kasumigaseki Station was only two stops from my hotel. I had no trouble getting there, and I waited for Daisuke. However, he seemed to be late. Then, my phone rang.

"I'm at Kasumigaseki Station! Where are you?" he said.

"I'm here, too!" I replied. We spent the next ten minutes looking for each other. Yet, I couldn't find him, so I sent him a picture of where I was.

That is when Daisuke figured it out. I was at Kasumigaseki Station near me in Saitama. He was at Kasumigaseki Station in Tokyo, near him… and closer to the airport. From this mistake, I learned that *jibun* has two meanings. In Osaka, it means "you," but in Tokyo it means "me!" I was so confused. However, like I said, I am careful. We planned to meet early, and the other Kasumigaseki Station was only about an hour away, so I was still able to see my friend and make my flight.

Notes

pick ~ up「車で~を迎えに行く」
see ~ off「~を見送る」
figure ~ out「~を理解する」

Take in the Article

A Today's Articleの内容と合うように、空所に適切な日本語を書き入れましょう。

	筆者	ダイスケ
待っていた場所	(¹.　　　　　　　) にある「かすみがせき駅」	(².　　　　　　　) にある「かすみがせき駅」
「自分」の意味	「(³.　　　　　　　)」の意味だと思った	「(⁴.　　　)」の意味で使った

B Today's Articleの内容と合っていればT、そうでなければFを選びましょう。また、問3では、Today's Articleの内容に関するTF問題を英語で作り、ペアで問題を出しあいましょう。

1. The writer thinks he is a very careful person.　　　　　　[T / F]

2. Daisuke couldn't meet the writer in the end.　　　　　　[T / F]

3. _____ [T / F]

C Today's Articleの内容と合うように、次の質問に英語で答えましょう。また、問3では、Today's Articleの内容に関する質問とその答えを英語で作り、ペアで問題を出しあいましょう。

1. **Q** How many days did the writer spend in Osaka?

　A _____

2. **Q** What did the writer do when he didn't find Daisuke at the station?

　A _____

3. **Q** _____

　A _____

Focus on the Signal

前に述べた内容と反対のことを言いたい場合には、but以外に **however** を用いることができます。however はbut とは異なり、文と文をつなげることはできません。また、however の直後にはカンマを付けることが多いです。

① I went to bed earlier than usual last night. **However**, I couldn't sleep well.

② I went to bed earlier than usual last night, **but** I couldn't sleep well.

「私は昨夜、いつもより早くベッドに入りました。**しかし**、あまり寝られませんでした」

however は文頭で用いることが多いですが、文中や文末でも用いられます。文頭で用いる場合と文中・文末で用いる場合で意味は変わりませんが、文中の場合は however の前後に、文末の場合は however の直前にカンマを付けることが多いです。

③ I recommended *sashimi* to him. He didn't try any, **however**.

「私は彼に刺し身を薦めました。**しかし**、彼は食べようとしませんでした」

however に似た表現に、**yet**、**still**、**nevertheless**、**on the contrary** などがあります。**yet** は「しかし」、**still** や **nevertheless** は「それでも」、**on the contrary** は「それどころか」に近いニュアンスで用いられます。いずれも文頭で用いることが多いです。

Use the Signal

A 空所に入る表現を a ~ c から選びましょう。

1. I wanted to use the coffee machine. However, (　　).

a. you shouldn't lie about an illness

2. It's April Fool's Day today. Yet, (　　).

b. we were out of beans

3. It is not hot today. On the contrary, (　　).

c. it is quite cold outside

B (　) 内の語句をヒントにして、次の日本語を英語で表現しましょう。

1. I am Japanese. しかし、知らない日本語がたくさんあります。
(however / Japanese words)

_____

2. His jokes are not so funny. それでも、私は彼の話が好きです。
(nevertheless)

_____

Opinions on the Article

A 記事に対するレンのコメントに合うように、下の表の空所を埋めましょう。

DL 08　CD 08

I have also misunderstood the names of places. When I was in the fifth grade, our class had a transfer student from Fuchu. I was surprised because my cousins lived in Fuchu, and I had been there many times. I told him everything I knew about the place. However, he did not understand at all. Then, I found out that my cousins lived in Fuchu in Tokyo, and the boy was from Fuchu in Hiroshima. There are many cities sharing the same name in Japan.

コメントの主旨	(¹.　　　　　) を勘違いした
具体的なエピソード	府中の話をしたが (².　　　　　) には通じなかった
理由	レンの (³.　　　　　) が住んでいたのは (⁴.　　　　　) の府中で、転入生が住んでいたのは (⁵.　　　　　) の府中だったから

B 表の内容と合うように、記事に対するリズのコメントの空所に入る語を選択肢から選びましょう。

DL 09　CD 09

コメントの主旨	日本語の表現の意味を勘違いした
具体的なエピソード	男性に駅で「すみません」と話しかけられ困惑した
理由	「すみません」は謝罪の言葉だと思っており、その男性は自分に対して何も悪いことをしていなかったから

I have also misunderstood the meaning of an (¹.　　　　　　　). Soon after I came to Japan, a (².　　　　　　　) said, "*Sumimasen*," to me at the (³.　　　　　　　). I was (⁴.　　　　　　　) because I thought that word means "I'm sorry." However, he had no reason to (⁵.　　　　　　　). Now, I know the word is used for more than apologies. It can also be "Excuse me" and "Thank you." Maybe he wanted to talk to me for some reason.

apologize　　confused　　expression　　man　　station

Express Your Opinions

日本語が生んだ勘違いについて、記事へのコメントを書きましょう。

A 前ページの表にならい、意見をまとめましょう。

コメントの主旨	
具体的なエピソード	
理由	

B 前ページのコメントにならい、上の表にまとめた内容を英語で書きましょう。

I have also misunderstood ( ). ＿＿＿＿

＿＿＿＿＿＿＿＿＿＿＿＿＿＿＿＿＿＿＿＿＿＿＿＿＿＿＿

＿＿＿＿＿＿＿＿＿＿＿＿＿＿＿＿＿＿＿＿＿＿＿＿＿＿＿

＿＿＿＿＿＿＿＿＿＿＿＿＿＿＿＿＿＿＿＿＿＿＿＿＿＿＿

＿＿＿＿＿＿＿＿＿＿＿＿＿＿＿＿＿＿＿＿＿＿＿＿＿＿＿

＿＿＿＿＿＿＿＿＿＿＿＿＿＿＿＿＿＿＿＿＿＿＿＿＿＿＿

☑ 使用した表現があればチェックをし、これまでのUnitで学んだ表現を使った場合は最後の□の横に書きましょう。

☐ however   ☐ nevertheless
☐ yet   ☐ on the contrary
☐ still   ☐

C ペアやグループで発表しましょう。

UNIT 3

Goodbye, old sweater!

ファストファッションか、長く着るか

反対の内容を先に伝える表現　**[(even) though]**

Important Expressions

🎧 DL 10　◎ CD 10

[　]内のアルファベットを並び替えて、下線部の日本語を表す英単語を完成させましょう。

1. 本と服のどちら**を**先に**取り出す**べきでしょうか。　　　　[a c k n p]（u _ _ _ _ _ ）

2. 5時間待たないといけないけれど、その**価値はあり**ます。　[h o r t]（w _ _ _ _ ）

3. その香りは、思っている以上にずっと長く**続き**ます。　　　[a s t]（l _ _ _ ）

4. 私はパーティー用の**衣装一式**を買わないといけません。　[f i t t u]（o _ _ _ _ _ ）

5. 私はチョコレートを食べ過ぎて、**罪悪感があり**ます。　　[i l t u y]（g _ _ _ _ _ ）

Signal Check

☐ で囲まれている日本語に対応する英語に〇をつけましょう。

1. Although it may be difficult, we have to choose one or the other.

それは難しいことかもしれない けれど 、私たちはどちらかを選ばないといけません。

2. Even though I bought three copies of the CD, I haven't listened to them yet.

私はそのCDを3枚買った のに 、まだ一度も聞いていません。

3. Despite the back pain, I had a good day today.

背中の痛みはありました が 、今日は良い一日でした。

Today's Article

次の投稿を読みましょう。

反対のことを先に言う表現に注意して読もう！

Question

@fashiongirl

Winter is around the corner, so I recently decided to unpack my winter clothes. However, when I took a close look at them, I was a little surprised. Even though I only wore them for one season, they looked a little worn out. I was really happy when I bought them because they were so cheap, but now I have to go shopping again. Should I give up on fast fashion?

Answer (2)

@diva

Yes! Fast fashion isn't worth it. The prices are low, but so is the quality. It's wasteful to throw clothes away after only one year. Although designer brands may seem expensive, they will last much longer. You will save money later because you won't have to go shopping so often. My mother always says, "Buy it nice or buy it twice."

@bobbybubble

I prefer fast fashion. I can buy several cheaper outfits instead of just one from an expensive brand. Also, despite their lower quality, some fast fashion clothes still look really nice. It's not a problem if they don't last long. When my cheap clothes start to look old, I can replace them with new, trending fashions every year. Waste doesn't have to be a problem either. Many stores will now take your old clothes for recycling, so you don't have to feel guilty! In my opinion, unless you find a really rare or special piece of clothing, you can have much more fun buying cheap new clothes every year.

Notes

around the corner「間近に」 worn out「着古された」 wasteful「無駄な」
replace A with B「AをBと入れ替える」

Take in the Article

A Today's Articleの内容と合うように、空所に適切な日本語を書き入れましょう。

	ファストファッション	デザイナーブランド
賛成のリプライ	@ (¹.　　　　　　　　　)	@ (².　　　　　　)
リプライ者の意見	・いろいろな服を購入できる ・(³.　　　　　　　) が、見た目が良いものもある ・買い換えがしやすい ・古い服はリサイクルに出せる	・(⁴.　　　　　　　　　) かもしれないが、長く持つ ・買い物に頻繁に行かなくてよいので、結果的に節約になる

B Today's Articleの内容と合っていればT、そうでなければFを選びましょう。また、問3では、Today's Articleの内容に関するTF問題を英語で作り、ペアで問題を出しあいましょう。

1. According to @diva's mother, we should buy an expensive brand item twice.　[T / F]

2. According to @bobbybubble, we should feel guilty for buying a lot of clothes.　[T / F]

3. _____　[T / F]

C Today's Articleの内容と合うように、次の質問に英語で答えましょう。また、問3では、Today's Articleの内容に関する質問とその答えを英語で作り、ペアで問題を出しあいましょう。

1. **Q** Does @diva think that the quality of fast fashion is low?

   A _____

2. **Q** Why was @fashiongirl surprised when she looked at her winter clothes?

   A _____

3. **Q** _____

   A _____

Focus on the Signal

主語・動詞を含む２つのかたまり（節）を **though**、**even though**、**although** などでつなげることで、「～だけれども…だ」「～（な）のに…だ」のように、１つの文の中で反対のことを同時に言うことができます。「～だけれども」の部分は、①のように先に置くことも、②のように後に置くこともできます。先に置く場合はカンマをつけるのが普通です。

① **(Even) though** my dog doesn't see well, he loves to look out the window.

② My dog loves to look out the window **(even) though** he doesn't see well.
　　「私の飼っている犬は目がよく見えない**けれども**、窓の外を見るのが好きです」

同じように、**despite** や **in spite of** を用いて、「～だけれども」「～にもかかわらず」というような反対の意味を表すこともできます。ただし、despite や in spite of を用いるのは、～が名詞や名詞のかたまり（名詞句・名詞節）で表現できる場合に限ります。③のように先に置くことも、④のように後に置くこともできます。先に置く場合は、句や節の終わりにカンマをつけるのが普通です。

③ **Despite** her busy schedule, Ann finished her tasks.

④ Ann finished her tasks **despite** her busy schedule.
　　「多忙なスケジュール**にもかかわらず**、アンは仕事を終えました」

Use the Signal

A 空所に入る表現を a ~ c から選びましょう。

1. Even though this was Ken's first contest, (　　).

2. Even though (　　), Mason danced well.

3. Despite (　　), James couldn't win the contest.

　　a. his efforts
　　b. his leg was hurting
　　c. his dance was better than the others

B （　　）内の語句をヒントにして、次の日本語を英語で表現しましょう。

1. どれくらいうまくいくか私には分からないけれど、やってみましょう。
　（ although / have no idea / how well it will work ）

_____

2. 彼女がいなくても、私たちはこの試合に勝たなければなりません。
　（ despite / absence / need to ）

_____

Opinions on the Article

A 投稿に対するトムのコメントに合うように、下の表の空所を埋めましょう。

DL 12　CD 12

@Tom

I prefer designer brands to fast fashion. Not only is it a waste of money and resources, I don't like the designs of fast fashion clothes. Because of mass production, they look really cheap. On the other hand, designer brands look high-quality. If you want to be regarded as a sophisticated person, you should choose designer brands.

好みのファッション	(¹.　　　　　　　　　　　　　　　　)
理由	ファストファッションはお金と (².　　　　　) の無駄であることに加えて、デザインが好きではない。(³.　　　　　　　) のため、とても安っぽく見える。一方デザイナーブランドには高級感がある。(⁴.　　　　　　　) 人として見られたいなら、デザイナーブランドを選ぶべき

B 表の内容と合うように、投稿に対するミオのコメントの空所に入る語句を選択肢から選びましょう。

DL 13　CD 13

好みのファッション	ファストファッション
理由1	平日に毎日違う服を着るために、最低でも毎シーズン5着は服が必要。一般的な大学生にはデザイナーブランドは高すぎる
理由2	ファッションの流行は目まぐるしく変化するので、前の年に買ったものが翌年には流行遅れになる。毎シーズン服を買いたい

@Mio

I prefer (¹.　　　　　　　　　　) to designer brands. I need at least five different outfits for each season so that I can dress (².　　　　　　　) on every weekday. Designer brands are too (³.　　　　　　　) for an ordinary university student. Additionally, because fashion trends change so rapidly, what I bought one year before goes out of (⁴.　　　　　　　) the next year. I want to buy new clothes every season.

differently　　expensive　　fast fashion　　style

Express Your Opinions

ファッションについて、投稿へのコメントを書きましょう。

A 前ページの表にならい、意見をまとめましょう。

好みのファッション	
理由	

B 前ページのコメントにならい、上の表にまとめた内容を英語で書きましょう。

I prefer ( ) to ( ).

_____

_____

_____

_____

_____

_____

☑ 使用した表現があればチェックをし、これまでのUnitで学んだ表現を使った場合は最後の□の横に書きましょう。

☐ though   ☐ despite

☐ even though   ☐ in spite of

☐ although   ☐

C ペアやグループで発表しましょう。

Home sweet home?

住めば都？

原因・理由を前や後ろにつなげる表現 **[because]**

Important Expressions

🎧 DL 14 ◎ CD 14

[ ] 内のアルファベットを並び替えて、下線部の日本語を表す英単語を完成させましょう。

1. <u>契約書</u>には何が書かれていましたか。　　　　[a c n o r t t]（c _ _ _ _ _ _ _）

2. ほとんどの人は、毎日10ドルの珈琲**を買う余裕があり**ません。 [d f f o r]（a _ _ _ _ _）

3. この家には、<u>広々とした</u>キッチン付きのダイニングルームがあります。

　　　　　　　　　　　　　　　　　　　　　[a c i o p s u]（s _ _ _ _ _ _ _）

4. そのドアに**オート**ロックを付けるべきです。　　[a c i m o t t u]（a _ _ _ _ _ _ _ _）

5. これ以上、**通学**に時間を費やしたくありません。　　[e m m o t u]（c _ _ _ _ _ _）

Signal Check

☐ で囲まれている日本語に対応する英語に〇をつけましょう。

1. Because Henry isn't a member of this team, he can't sit on the bench with the players.

ヘンリーはこのチームのメンバーではない ので 、選手と一緒にベンチに座ることはできません。

2. You look like sisters because you are wearing the same jacket.

同じジャケットを着ている から 、姉妹みたいに見えますよ。

3. As it is late, I will watch the movie tomorrow.

もう遅い から 、その映画を見るのは明日にします。

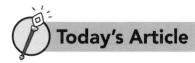

Today's Article

DL 15　CD 15

次のブログを読みましょう。

原因や理由を述べる表現に注意して読もう！

I need to move!

June 3, 2023 at 1:25 p.m.

I hate my current apartment. It's noisy all the time because it's right next to a busy street. I can't even hear my TV if I open my window to get fresh air. Since I only have a few months left in the contract, I started looking for a new place.

As I am still a university student, I can't afford an expensive place. However, I did find two affordable places in quiet areas that might be good for me. The first one is close to my university. Actually, it's only a few minutes away on foot! Super convenient, right? If I move there, I won't have to worry about the train at all. However, this apartment is old and kind of small. I don't think it's big enough to invite my university friends over to hang out.

The second place is very different. It's newer and much more spacious. It would be a very comfortable place to party and drink with my friends. Because it has automatic locks, and it's on the third floor, it's also a safer place. Sounds perfect, right? Well, this apartment is cheap because of its location. The nearest station is 20 minutes away on foot, and the university is 40 minutes away by train. Because of this, I would have to wake up an hour earlier every day and waste two hours commuting.

I should make a decision soon, but I don't know what to do. Does anyone have any advice? Please leave me a comment below.

Notes

kind of「少し」
hang out「遊ぶ」

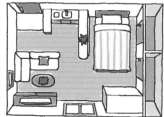

Take in the Article

A Today's Articleの内容と合うように、空所に適切な日本語を書き入れましょう。

	1つ目の候補	2つ目の候補
部屋の広さ	(1.　　　　　　　　)	(2.　　　　　　　　　　　)
大学への通学時間	徒歩で (3.　　) 分	徒歩と電車で (4.　　) 分

B Today's Articleの内容と合っていればT、そうでなければFを選びましょう。また、問3では、Today's Articleの内容に関するTF問題を英語で作り、ペアで問題を出しあいましょう。

1. The writer thinks the first place is convenient because she doesn't have to use the train to go to her university.　　　　　　　　　　　[T / F]

2. The second place is too small to hold a party there.　　　　　[T / F]

3. ＿＿＿＿＿＿＿＿＿＿＿＿＿＿＿＿＿＿＿＿＿＿＿＿＿ [T / F]

C Today's Articleの内容と合うように、次の質問に英語で答えましょう。また、問3では、Today's Articleの内容に関する質問とその答えを英語で作り、ペアで問題を出しあいましょう。

1. Q Is the writer thinking of moving now?

A ＿＿＿＿＿＿＿＿＿＿＿＿＿＿＿＿＿＿＿＿＿＿＿＿＿＿＿

2. Q Why does the writer think that the second place is safer than the first one?

A ＿＿＿＿＿＿＿＿＿＿＿＿＿＿＿＿＿＿＿＿＿＿＿＿＿＿＿

3. Q ＿＿＿＿＿＿＿＿＿＿＿＿＿＿＿＿＿＿＿＿＿＿＿＿＿＿＿

A ＿＿＿＿＿＿＿＿＿＿＿＿＿＿＿＿＿＿＿＿＿＿＿＿＿＿＿

Focus on the Signal

「〜（な）ので」「〜（だ）から」など、原因や理由を表したいときは、**because** を用いることができます。

① I used a printed dictionary **because** my PC wasn't working.
　「パソコンが作動しなかった**ので**、紙の辞書を使いました」

②のように理由を文の前半に持ってくることも、③のように理由を文の後半に持ってくることもできます。②の場合は、節の終わりにカンマをつけるのが普通です。③の場合、becauseの前にカンマをつけません。結果に重点が置かれる場合は②、原因・理由が大切な情報である場合は③の形を用いる場合が多いです。

② **Because** my sister is noisy, I wake up at 8:30 on Sundays.

③ I wake up at 8:30 on Sundays **because** my sister is noisy.
　「妹がうるさい**ので**、日曜日は8時半に起きてしまいます」

becauseと同じように、**as** や **since** を使うこともできます。また、似たような意味で **because of** を使うこともできますが、because ofの後は主語＋動詞ではなく、名詞や名詞のかたまり（名詞句・名詞節）を置きます。

④ **Because of** the rain, I couldn't take my dog on a walk.
　「雨**のせいで**、飼い犬を散歩に連れて行くことができませんでした」

Use the Signal

A 空所に入る表現をa〜cから選びましょう。

1. I was absent from school for a while because
　（　　　　）.

2. Because I had nothing to do, （　　　　）.

3. As （　　　　）, I asked him to take out the garlic.

　a. I don't like the flavor
　b. I had a fever
　c. I kept looking at Twitter

B （　　　）内の語句をヒントにして、次の日本語を英語で表現しましょう。

1. 友だちが参加するので、私もパーティーに行きます。
　(my friends / join / as well)

　_____

2. 彼の冗談のせいで、上司の機嫌は悪かったです。
　(his joke / in a bad mood)

　_____

Opinions on the Article

A ブログに対するレンのコメントに合うように、下の表の空所を埋めましょう。

🎧 DL 16 💿 CD 16

 Ren I think you should choose the first option. Since you are a university student, you should live near the university. You can spend as much time as you want studying at the university because you don't have to spend much time commuting. Time is money. Also, it will make it easier for you to hang out with your friends because many of them probably live close to the university, too.

おすすめの物件	(1.　　　　　　　　) の物件
理由1	(2.　　　　　　) に多くの時間を使う必要がないので、好きなだけ大学で勉強できる
理由2	(3.　　　　　　　　　) もおそらく大学の近くに住んでいるので、彼らと (4.　　　　　) ことがより簡単にできる

B 表の内容と合うように、ブログに対するリズのコメントの空所に入る語を選択肢から選びましょう。

🎧 DL 17 💿 CD 17

おすすめの物件	2つ目の物件
理由1	住環境は健康のために重要なので、快適と思う部屋に住むべき
理由2	新しくてきれいな部屋なら、より集中して課題に取り組める
理由3	本を読む、音楽を聴くなど、通学時間を使う方法はたくさんある

Liz I think you should choose the (1.　　　　　　　　　) option. Since the (2.　　　　　　　　　) you live in is important for your health, you should live where you feel (3.　　　　　　　　). If your room is new and clean, you will be able to concentrate more on your (4.　　　　　　　　). Two hours of commuting is not a problem because there are many ways to spend the time, such as reading books and listening to music.

assignments　　comfortable　　environment　　second

Express Your Opinions

どちらの物件を選ぶべきかについて、ブログへのコメントを書きましょう。

A 前ページの表にならい、意見をまとめましょう。

おすすめの物件	
理由	

B 前ページのコメントにならい、上の表にまとめた内容を英語で書きましょう。

I think you should choose the (　　　　　) option. ＿＿＿＿＿＿

＿＿＿＿＿＿＿＿＿＿＿＿＿＿＿＿＿＿＿＿＿＿＿

＿＿＿＿＿＿＿＿＿＿＿＿＿＿＿＿＿＿＿＿＿＿＿

＿＿＿＿＿＿＿＿＿＿＿＿＿＿＿＿＿＿＿＿＿＿＿

＿＿＿＿＿＿＿＿＿＿＿＿＿＿＿＿＿＿＿＿＿＿＿

＿＿＿＿＿＿＿＿＿＿＿＿＿＿＿＿＿＿＿＿＿＿＿

☑ 使用した表現があればチェックをし、これまでのUnitで学んだ表現を使った場合は最後の□の横に書きましょう。

☐ because 　　　　　　　　☐ because of

☐ as 　　　　　　　　　　☐

☐ since

C ペアやグループで発表しましょう。

Will you be my girlfriend? Check □ Yes or □ No

想いは直接伝えるか

 理由と主張を並べる表現 [so / therefore]

Important Expressions

🎧 DL 18　💿 CD 18

[　]内のアルファベットを並び替えて、下線部の日本語を表す英単語を完成させましょう。

1. 子どもの頃からジェットコースターが**怖い**です。　　　　[a c d e r]（s _ _ _ _ _ ）

2. このニュースは**全くの**デマです。　　　　　　　　　　[a l l o t y]（t _ _ _ _ _ _ ）

3. 彼は私がそれをすべきだと**提案し**ました。　　　　　　[e g g s t u]（s _ _ _ _ _ _ ）

4. **気まずい**沈黙がその場に流れました。　　　　　　　　[a d k r w w]（a _ _ _ _ _ _ ）

5. それは本当に**ひどい**アイデアですね。　　　　　　　　[b e e i l r r]（t _ _ _ _ _ _ _ ）

Signal Check

☐ で囲まれている日本語に対応する英語に○をつけましょう。

1. Students are on spring break, so the train is empty.

学生が春休み中 だから 、電車がガラガラです。

2. Hairstyles are not related to behavior. Therefore, the school rule should be abolished.

髪型と素行は関係がありません。 それゆえ 、その校則は撤廃されるべきです。

3. I have hay fever. That is why I hate spring and autumn.

私は花粉症なのです。 そういう訳で 、春と秋は嫌いです。

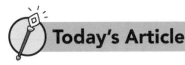

Today's Article

次の投稿を読みましょう。

理由と主張を並べる表現に注意して読もう！

Question

@lovesick

Oh kind and wise people of the internet, I need your help. I met an amazing girl this year at my university. We have a few classes together, so we see each other often. At first, we started sending text messages to each other to talk about assignments. Now, we sometimes hang out together with other classmates. I really like her, so I want to ask her to be my girlfriend, but I'm scared of messing everything up. First of all, she's totally out of my league. She's beautiful, smart, and fun, and I'm just a plain, boring guy. Only my mother says I'm handsome. However, I can't stop thinking about her, so I have to try, right? The problem is that I don't know what to say or how to say it.

My friend suggested I express my feelings in a text message. I could write my message carefully, and she could have time to think about her reply. Therefore, it would be easiest for everyone. Also, we won't have to look at each other in awkward silence if she says no.

However, my brother thinks that's a terrible idea. He says that showing her how I feel is the most important thing, which is why I should do it face-to-face. He also says that telling her in person would make me look cool and brave. I'm sure that this way is more romantic, but it's also scarier. That is why I need your advice. What should I do?

Notes

mess ~ up「～を台無しにする」
out of my league「高嶺の花、手の届かない」
in person「直接会って」

34

Take in the Article

A **Today's Article**の内容と合うように、空所に適切な日本語を書き入れましょう。

	友達の提案		兄の提案	
告白の方法	(¹.) で伝える		(².) で伝える	
その方法の利点	・メッセージを (³.) に書くことができ、相手も返事を考える時間が持てる ・断られたときに、気まずい雰囲気にならずに済む		・かっこよくて (⁴.) 　に見える ・ロマンチックである	

B **Today's Article**の内容と合っていればT、そうでなければFを選びましょう。また、問3では、**Today's Article**の内容に関するTF問題を英語で作り、ペアで問題を出しあいましょう。

1. The writer doesn't know the girl's contact information. 　　[T / F]

2. For the writer, his brother's idea is scarier than his friend's idea. 　　[T / F]

3. _____ [T / F]

C **Today's Article**の内容と合うように、次の質問に英語で答えましょう。また、問3では、**Today's Article**の内容に関する質問とその答えを英語で作り、ペアで問題を出しあいましょう。

1. **Q** Does the writer's brother suggest that he tell the girl directly?

   A _____

2. **Q** Where does the writer usually see the girl?

   A _____

3. **Q** _____

   A _____

Focus on the Signal

「～（だ）から」「～（な）ので」など、原因・理由に続けて結果や主張を言いたい場合には、**so**を用いることができます。

① I didn't have time to do my hair, **so** I'm wearing this cap today.
  「髪をセットする時間がなかったので、今日はこのキャップを被っています」

soは、前の文にカンマで続けて使うことができます。③のように、文の最初に**So**をつけるのは、会話文などのカジュアルな場面に限定されます。ライティングでは、文頭でSoを用いない方が適切です。

② ○ I have reached the data limit, **so** I can't watch YouTube videos without Wi-Fi.

③ △ I have reached the data limit. **So** I can't watch YouTube videos without Wi-Fi.
  「通信制限がかかっているので、Wi-FiなしではYouTubeを見られません」

soに似た表現に、**therefore**、**this is why**、**that is why**、**thus**、**accordingly**、**for these reasons** などがあります。いずれもsoよりやや堅い表現で、「それゆえ」「したがって」「その結果」などの日本語に近いニュアンスであることが多いです。これらの表現は、②のように、直前でカンマを用いて文と文をつなげることはできません。また、④のように、**and**だけでも日本語の「～（し）て…」のような軽い因果関係を表すことができます。

④ Meg played peekaboo, **and** her child stopped crying.
  「メグはいないいないばあをして、子どもは泣き止みました」

Use the Signal

A 空所に入る表現をa～cから選びましょう。

1. There was no soy sauce left, so (　　). 　　a. I put on a little soy sauce
2. His food didn't have any taste, so (　　). 　　b. I didn't need chopsticks
3. I had sandwiches for today's lunch, so (　　). 　c. I ate it without adding any

B （　　）内の語句をヒントにして、次の日本語を英語で表現しましょう。

1. 私は昨日、徹夜でレポートを書いていたので、今は眠いです。
  (all night yesterday / so)

  _____

2. I think this problem is important. それゆえ、彼女の提案には賛成です。
  (therefore / agree with / suggestion)

  _____

Opinions on the Article

A 投稿に対するトムのコメントに合うように、下の表の空所を埋めましょう。

 DL 20 CD 20

 @Tom I think you should express your feelings in a text message. Expressing your love is a huge event for both of you, so it must be perfect. As your friend says, if you choose to send a text message, you can take as much time as you want for preparation and choose words of love carefully. Also, a sophisticated message will make you look smart and polite.

おすすめの告白方法	(1.) で伝える
理由1	準備に (2.) 時間をかけて、(3.) を慎重に選ぶことができる
理由2	(4.) メッセージを送ることで、賢く (5.) 印象を与えることができる

B 表の内容と合うように、投稿に対するミオのコメントの空所に入る語を選択肢から選びましょう。

DL 21 CD 21

おすすめの告白方法	直接会って伝える
理由1	告白される女の子の立場から言えば、なぜ好きかよりもどれだけ好きかを伝えるほうが大切であり、テキストメッセージでは情熱は伝わらない
理由2	相手の気持ちを読み取れるので、必要ならば言葉を付け足したり変えたりすることができる

@Mio I think you should express your feelings (1.   ). From the standpoint of a girl being asked out, showing someone how much you love them is more (2.   ) than telling them why you love them. You won't be able to convey your (3.   ) with a text message. Moreover, because you can read her (4.   ), you can add and change your words if (5.   ).

face-to-face   feelings   important   necessary   passion

Express Your Opinions

告白の方法について、投稿へのコメントを書きましょう。

A 前ページの表にならい、意見をまとめましょう。

おすすめの告白方法	
理由	

B 前ページのコメントにならい、上の表にまとめた内容を英語で書きましょう。

I think you should express your feelings (　　　　　　　　　　　　).

_____

_____

_____

_____

_____

_____

✔️ 使用した表現があればチェックをし、これまでのUnitで学んだ表現を使った場合は最後の□の横に書きましょう。

☐ so ☐ accordingly
☐ therefore ☐ for these reasons
☐ this is why / that is why ☐
☐ thus

C ペアやグループで発表しましょう。

When is the wedding?

初めてのデートプラン

 順番に並べて伝える表現 **[first, second, finally]**

Important Expressions

🎧 DL 22 💿 CD 22

[　]内のアルファベットを並び替えて、下線部の日本語を表す英単語を完成させましょう。

1. 私は彼に**プロポーズし**ようと思っています。　　[e o o p r s]（p _ _ _ _ _ _）

2. シュンは**静かに**座って、ニュースを見ていました。　[e i l t u y]（q _ _ _ _ _ _）

3. **できる**だけ外で遊びましょう。　　　　　　　　　[b e i l o s s]（p _ _ _ _ _ _ _）

4. 私の部屋は**散らかって**います。　　　　　　　　　　[e s s y]（m _ _ _ _）

5. **大丈夫**ですよ、ありがとう。　　　　　　　　　　　　[e i n]（f _ _ _）

Signal Check

　で囲まれている日本語に対応する英語に○をつけましょう。

1. First, don't take caffeine before going to bed.

まず、寝る前にカフェインを取らないようにしましょう。

2. Second, don't use your smartphone in bed.

次に、ベッドの中でスマホを使わないようにしましょう。

3. Finally, slowly take a deep breath. This should help you sleep well.

最後に、ゆっくりと深呼吸しましょう。よく眠れるはずです。

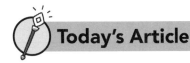 **Today's Article**

🎧 DL 23　◉ CD 23

次のテキストメッセージのやり取りを読みましょう。

 順番に並べて伝える表現に注意して読もう！

Dan (18:30): Hey Masa, did you ask Yuki to be your girlfriend yet?

Masa (18:32): Not yet, but I did ask her out on a date, and she said yes!

Kazuki (18:35): That's great! Where are you going to take her?

Masa (18:36): I'm still not sure. Maybe Disneyland?

Dan (18:37): For the first date?! That's too much.

Kazuki (18:37): LOL. Yeah, man. Save that for later.

Masa (18:38): Really? What should I do then?

Dan (18:43): If you want to have a fun date, how about this? First, take her to see a movie. The new Punchman movie is great. Second, spend some time at a game center. Win her something from a claw machine if you can. Finally, have dinner together. Just don't propose yet. Haha.

Kazuki (18:45): A movie for a first date? I don't think that's a good idea.

Masa (18:46): Why not?

Kazuki (18:50): You will be sitting quietly for about two hours without talking. On the first date, you should get to know each other as much as possible, so how about this? Go to a café first. They are great places for sweets and conversation. Girls love both. Second, go to a restaurant, but make sure the food is easy to eat. I mean, find something that isn't messy. After dinner, have a few drinks at a bar, or just go for a long walk.

Masa (18:52): Hmm... That sounds simple. But what if we run out of things to talk about?

Dan (18:53): That's why my plan is better! You'll have fun things to do.

Kazuki (18:54): No! No movie! You'll be fine! Just don't be shy.

Notes

ask ~ out「～をデートに誘う」　LOL「(笑)(laugh out loudの略語)」　claw machine「クレーンゲーム」
make sure「～を確認する」　run out of ~「～が尽きる」

Take in the Article

A Today's Articleの内容と合うように、空所に適切な日本語を書き入れましょう。

	最初に行く場所	次に行く場所	その後のプラン
ダンの提案	(1.　　　　　　　)	(2.　　　　　　　　　　)	食事をする
カズキの提案	(3.　　　　　　　)	(4.　　　　　　　　　　)	バーに行くか散歩をする

B Today's Articleの内容と合っていればT、そうでなければFを選びましょう。また、問3では、Today's Articleの内容に関するTF問題を英語で作り、ペアで問題を出しあいましょう。

1. Neither Dan nor Kazuki thinks that it's good to go to Disneyland on a first date.
[T / F]

2. According to Dan's idea, Masa should go to a game center before watching a movie.
[T / F]

3. _____ [T / F]

C Today's Articleの内容と合うように、次の質問に英語で答えましょう。また、問3では、Today's Articleの内容に関する質問とその答えを英語で作り、ペアで問題を出しあいましょう。

1. Q Who suggests that Masa should talk with Yuki a lot?

A _____

2. Q What does Kazuki tell Masa to make sure of when going to a restaurant?

A _____

3. Q _____

A _____

Focus on the Signal

「1つ目に、…。2つ目に、…。3つ目に、…。」や「まず、…。次に、…。そして、…。」のように、複数の内容を順序立てて言いたい場合には、**First, ... Second, ... Third, ...** という表現を用いることができます。これらは普通、文頭で用います。

① Making banana juice is easy. **First,** put some banana and some milk in a blender. **Second,** blend them well.

> 「バナナジュースを作るのは簡単です。**まず、**バナナと牛乳をミキサーに入れます。**次に、**よく混ぜます」

「2つ目に」の代わりに、「**次に**」を意味する **Next** を用いることもできます。また、「**最後に**」と言いたい場合には、**Last(ly)** や **Finally** などを用いることができます。

② **First,** it is economical. **Next,** it is a universal design. **Finally,** it is eco-friendly.

> 「**まず、**それは経済的です。**次に、**それはユニバーサルデザインです。**最後に、**それは環境に優しいです」

複数の理由を述べる場合には、1つ目の理由を述べる前に、There are three reasons for this.「この理由は3つあります」のような前置きを置くと、読み手・聞き手にとってその後の展開が分かりやすくなります。

Use the Signal

A 次の1〜3の表現が入る箇所を a〜d から選びましょう。なお、英文の文頭は全て大文字で示してあります。

This bag is better for three reasons. **[a]** The design and color are cool. **[b]** It is big enough to put many things in. **[c]** It can carry many textbooks. **[d]** It has a drink holder, which is very useful.

1. First, （　　） **2.** Next, （　　） **3.** Finally, （　　）

B （　　）内の語句をヒントにして、次の日本語を英語で表現しましょう。

1. You can try to save money in many ways. まず、マイボトルを持ち歩きましょう。(your own water bottle)

_____

2. I want to be a media creator. 理由は2つあります。

_____

Opinions on the Article

A レンによるデートプランの提案に合うように、下の表の空所を埋めましょう。

🎧 DL 24　💿 CD 24

Ren (19:15): If you want to have a fun date, how about going for a drive? First, rent a car and go pick her up. Second, decide the destination. I recommend you choose where to go together. You should prepare several choices: going to the sea or going to the mountains, for example. Finally, enjoy the driving date! You can see beautiful sights and never run out of things to talk about.

レンの提案	ドライブデート
最初にすること	車を借りて彼女を (**1.** 　　　　　　) 行く
次にすること	彼女と2人で (**2.** 　　　　　) を決める ※いくつか (**3.** 　　　　　) を準備しておくとよい
その後のプラン	ドライブを楽しむ。(**4.** 　　　　　　　　　　) が見られるので、 (**5.** 　　　　　　) ことはない

B 表の内容と合うように、リズによるデートプランの提案の空所に入る語を選択肢から選びましょう。

🎧 DL 25　💿 CD 25

リズの提案	ショッピングデート
最初にすること	ショッピングモールの最寄り駅で待ち合わせする ※遅くとも待ち合わせの10分前には行くこと
次にすること	ショッピングモール内のレストランで昼食を食べる
その後のプラン	商品を見て歩きながら互いのファッションの好みや趣味の話をする

Liz (19:30): If you want to have a fun date, how about going (**1.** 　　　　　)? First, (**2.** 　　　　　) her at the station near a shopping mall. You should go there at (**3.** 　　　　) 10 minutes early. Don't make a girl wait. (**4.** 　　　　　), eat lunch at a restaurant in the mall. Finally, go window-shopping at the mall. You can talk about each other's fashion taste and (**5.** 　　　　　) while shopping.

hobbies　least　meet　second　shopping

Express Your Opinions

マサへのデートプランの提案を書きましょう。

A 前ページの表にならい、意見をまとめましょう。

あなたの提案	
最初にすること	
次にすること	
その後のプラン	

B 前ページの提案にならい、上の表にまとめた内容を英語で書きましょう。

（　　：　　）: If you want to have a fun date, how about

（　　　　　　　　　　　　　） ? _____

_____

_____

_____

_____

_____

☑ 使用した表現があればチェックをし、これまでのUnitで学んだ表現を使った場合は最後の□の横に書きましょう。

- ☐ First,
- ☐ Second,
- ☐ Third,
- ☐ Next,

- ☐ Last(ly),
- ☐ Finally,
- ☐

C ペアやグループで発表しましょう。

We'll have the best food stall at the festival.

人気店の秘訣

言いたいことを足していく表現 **[also]**

Important Expressions

🎧 DL 26　◎ CD 26

[　]内のアルファベットを並び替えて、下線部の日本語を表す英単語を完成させましょう。

1. 毎週通うタイ料理の<u>屋台</u>があります。　　　　　　[allt]（s＿＿＿＿）

2. そのニュースはより多くの関心<u>を引き付け</u>ます。　[acrttt]（a＿＿＿＿＿＿）

3. このマスクは<u>布</u>で作りました。　　　　　　　　[abcir]（f＿＿＿＿＿）

4. 君と君の弟の声<u>を区別する</u>ことができません。

　　　　　　　　　　　　　[ghiiinsstu]（d＿＿＿＿＿＿＿＿＿＿）

5. 彼は文化祭実行<u>委員会</u>の一員です。　[eeimmott]（c＿＿＿＿＿＿＿＿）

Signal Check

☐☐で囲まれている日本語に対応する英語に〇をつけましょう。

1. This bed is inexpensive. It can also be used as a sofa.

このベッドはお手頃です。 それに 、ソファとして も 使えます。

2. You should read these instructions. Moreover, you need to sign the documents.

この説明書を読んでください。 さらに 、書類への署名が必要です。

3. There are about 100 convenience stores in this city. In addition, more than 10 new branches are scheduled to open this year.

この町にはおよそ100軒のコンビニがあります。 その上 、10を超える新店舗が今年開店予定です。

 **Today's Article**

DL 27　CD 27

次のオンラインチャットのやり取りを読みましょう。

 言いたいことを足していく表現に注意して読もう！

 T-kun 16:42
Hello, everyone! It's time to start planning our food stall for this year's school festival. Last year, we switched from fried chicken to french fries, and I think that worked out very well. The fries were also easier to store and cook than chicken, so I think we should do that again. However, I think other stalls did better than us last year. Does anyone have any new ideas about how to attract more people?

Tetsu-G 18:02
I think we should make our display look better. Last year, we just wrote on cardboard with markers, and it didn't look very nice. Moreover, it was hard to read from a distance. I think we should make our signs out of fabric instead of paper. It will be a little more expensive at first, but it will look better! Additionally, we can reuse them next year!

 Ami-chan 18:31
I think we should all wear matching aprons this year. People will be able to distinguish staff and guests more easily. Plus, our clothes won't get dirty. In addition, it will make our booth look more fun!

 Megu 18:56
Can we play music at our booth? That would be fun too, right?

 T-kun 19:12
Megu, that might be difficult. If every booth is allowed to play their own music, the festival will be really noisy. I don't think the visitors will like that. Also, the festival committee might be planning to use the school's speakers to play music throughout the campus. I'll check, though!
Thanks, everyone! Let's vote on these ideas at our next meeting!

Notes

switch from A to B「AからBへ変える」　work out「うまくいく」　from a distance「遠くから」
make A out of B「BからAを作る」

Take in the Article

A Today's Articleの内容と合うように、空所に適切な日本語を書き入れましょう。

	昨年はどうしたか	今年に向けた提案
料理	(¹.)	(².)
ディスプレイ	(³.) で作った	(⁴.) で作るのが良い

B Today's Articleの内容と合っていればT、そうでなければFを選びましょう。また、問3では、Today's Articleの内容に関するTF問題を英語で作り、ペアで問題を出しあいましょう。

1. They had their own food stall both last year and two years ago.　　　[T / F]

2. T-kun gives two reasons why every booth can't play their own music.　[T / F]

3. _____ [T / F]

C Today's Articleの内容と合うように、次の質問に英語で答えましょう。また、問3では、Today's Articleの内容に関する質問とその答えを英語で作り、ペアで問題を出しあいましょう。

1. **Q** Why does Tetsu-G think that using fabric signs can save money?

   A _____

2. **Q** Give three reasons why they should wear matching aprons.

   A _____

   _____

   _____

3. **Q** _____

   A _____

Focus on the Signal

「それに」「さらに」「その上」「また」など、言いたいことを足していく場合、**also**を用いることができます。also は文頭に置くことも、文中に置くこともできます。文中に置く場合、be動詞の後ろや一般動詞の前に置くのが普通です。

① I want to go to a café today. **Also**, I want to go buy new shoes.

② I want to go to a café today. I **also** want to go buy new shoes.

「今日はカフェに行きたいです。**それに**、新しい靴も買いに行きたいです」

同じような表現に、**in addition**、**plus**、**moreover**、**furthermore**、**additionally**、**similarly** などがあります。いずれも文頭で使います。moreover は also と同じように文中に置くこともよくありますが、その場合は前後をカンマで区切ることが多いです。

③ The shop's interior is relaxing. **Moreover**, the music is nice and easy to listen to.

④ The shop's interior is relaxing. The music, **moreover**, is nice and easy to listen to.

「そのお店のインテリアは落ち着きます。**それに**、音楽がすてきで聴き心地が良いのです」

似たような表現に、and や then がありますが、書き言葉ではand を文頭で使わないようにしましょう。また、then や and then は基本的に時間的な順序を表すため、上記の表現と混同しないように注意しましょう。

Use the Signal

A 空所に入る表現を a ~ c から選びましょう。

1. I like the story of this movie. Also, (　　　　).

2. In the hotel, the coffee was free, and also, (　　　).

3. The waiter got my order wrong. Also, (　　　).

a. the actors gave great performances

b. we were able to read newspapers

c. the food wasn't hot enough

B (　　) 内の語句をヒントにして、次の日本語を英語で表現しましょう。

1. I have to buy a necktie. それに、スーツも新調しないといけません。
(also / get a new suit)

_____

2. 私の兄はいつも他の人のことを気にかけていて、礼儀正しいです。
(cares about / also / polite)

_____

Opinions on the Article

A 学園祭の出店に関するトムの提案に合うように、下の表の空所を埋めましょう。

🎧 DL 28　◉ CD 28

> **Tom 19:30** I think we should offer several flavors of french fries. Last year, we just sold salt and pepper flavor. If we offer more flavors such as consommé, cheese, and sesame, customers can share different flavors with their friends. This will attract many customers. Moreover, one customer may buy two or more flavors. In addition, it won't be troublesome to offer several flavors because we just need to add seasoning to the fries.

提案の内容	いくつかの (¹.　　　　) のフライドポテトを提供する
理由1	友人と違う味を (².　　　　　) できるので、お客さんが増える
理由2	１人のお客さんが複数の味を買うかもしれない
理由3	フライドポテトに (³.　　　　　) を (⁴.　　　　　) だけなので (⁵.　　　　　) ではない

B 表の内容と合うように、学園祭の出店に関するミオの提案の空所に入る語を選択肢から選びましょう。

🎧 DL 29　◉ CD 29

提案の内容	再利用可能な入れ物でフライドポテトを提供する
理由1	カラフルで派手な入れ物は映えるし、若者に人気になるだろう
理由2	入れ物のごみを減らすことができる。また入れ物を返した人にいくらか返金するようにすれば、入れ物を捨てる人はいないだろう

> **Mio 19:45** I think we should offer french fries with (¹.　　　　　　) bowls. If we offer the fries in colorful, fancy bowls, it will be great for pictures, so (².　　　　　　) will like it. Also, we can reduce the (³.　　　　　　) of bowls. Last year, we had to discard a lot of used paper bowls, but we won't have to worry about that. Plus, if we (⁴.　　　　　　) some money to those who bring their bowls back to our stall, they won't (⁵.　　　　　　) them away.

return　　reusable　　teenagers　　throw　　waste

Express Your Opinions

学園祭の出店について、提案を書きましょう。

A 前ページの表にならい、意見をまとめましょう。

提案の内容	
理由	

B 前ページの提案にならい、上の表にまとめた内容を英語で書きましょう。

（　　：　　）: I think we should （

）._____

_____

_____

_____

_____

☑ 使用した表現があればチェックをし、これまでのUnitで学んだ表現を使った場合は最後の□の横に書きましょう。

- ☐ also
- ☐ in addition
- ☐ plus
- ☐ moreover

- ☐ furthermore
- ☐ additionally
- ☐ similarly
- ☐

C ペアやグループで発表しましょう。

UNIT 8

It's just a little white lie.

ウソをつくのは悪いこと？

仮定の話をする表現　[if]

Important Expressions

🎧 DL 30　💿 CD 30

[　]内のアルファベットを並び替えて、下線部の日本語を表す英単語を完成させましょう。

1. 彼は目を伏せて、**正直に**話しました。　　　　　　[e l n o s t y]（h _ _ _ _ _ _ _ ）

2. 私は6時に起きようとしますが、たいてい**寝坊し**ます。
　　　　　　　　　　　　　　　　　[e e e l p r s v]（o _ _ _ _ _ _ _ _ ）

3. 彼の仕事ぶり**に感謝して**います。　　　[a c e e i p p r t]（a _ _ _ _ _ _ _ _ _ ）

4. そのニュースを聞いて**落胆し**ました。　[a c d e g i o r s u]（d _ _ _ _ _ _ _ _ _ _ ）

5. **前の**アカウントはもう消しました。　　　　[e i o r s u v]（p _ _ _ _ _ _ _ ）

Signal Check

　　　で囲まれている日本語に対応する英語に〇をつけましょう。

1. If you are free this evening, would you like to go to a movie with me?
　　もし 今日の午後暇 なら 、私と一緒に映画に行きませんか。

2. What should I do if I don't have my dictionary?
　　辞書がない 場合は どうしたらよいですか。

3. I will buy this new smartphone even if it's expensive.
　　たとえ 値段が高い としても 、この新しいスマホを買います。

Today's Article

次の記事を読みましょう。

 仮定の話をする表現に注意して読もう！

By Samantha Wilson

September 20, 2023 at 5:00 p.m.

I recently watched a movie about a world with no lies. Everyone in the story spoke honestly, even if the things they said were very rude. It was hilarious, but it made me think about how often we tell lies. We teach children that lying is wrong. Yet, we lie to our friends and family all the time to avoid problems or to make them happy. Is that OK, or is that wrong, too? Are some lies good? If so, which ones?

If you oversleep and miss a test at school, what would you tell the teacher? If you are honest, the teacher might be strict and give you a zero. However, if you say you have a fever, the teacher might let you take the test on a different day. Is this kind of lie bad?

Here is another situation. Recently, my boyfriend started knitting a hat for me. Naturally, I appreciate the effort he put into it, but it isn't my style. Will I tell him that? No way! I will say, "I love it! It's my new favorite hat!" I will lie to him to make him happy. Otherwise, he might get discouraged and stop knitting. Also, I learned from my previous mistakes. My last boyfriend was not very good at cooking. One time, he made dinner for me and asked me about the taste. I decided that I should be honest, or he would not improve. We had a fight and broke up because of that, but was I wrong for telling the truth?

Notes

hilarious「とても面白い」
naturally「当然、もちろん」
put effort into ~「~に努力を注ぐ」
break up「（カップルが）別れる」

Take in the Article

A Today's Articleの内容と合うように、空所に適切な日本語を書き入れましょう。

	本当のことを言う	嘘をつく
試験に遅刻した	(1.　　　　　　　　　) かもしれない	(2.　　　　　　　　　) かもしれない
ニット帽が好みでない	(3.　　　　　　) して (4.　　　　　) かもしれない	喜ぶだろう

B Today's Articleの内容と合っていればT、そうでなければFを選びましょう。また、問3では、Today's Articleの内容に関するTF問題を英語で作り、ペアで問題を出しあいましょう。

1. The writer believes we should be honest if we oversleep. [T / F]

2. The writer really likes the hat her boyfriend started knitting. [T / F]

3. _____ [T / F]

C Today's Articleの内容と合うように、次の質問に英語で答えましょう。また、問3では、Today's Articleの内容に関する質問とその答えを英語で作り、ペアで問題を出しあいましょう。

1. Q Did the characters in the movie tell many lies?

   A _____

2. Q Why did the writer and her last boyfriend have a fight and break up?

   A _____

3. Q _____

   A _____

Focus on the Signal

「もし〜なら」などと仮定の話をしたい場合には、**if** を用いることができます。

① **If** you want a part-time job, please contact us.
「もしアルバイトをお探しでしたら、我々に連絡してください」

「もし [たとえ] 〜だとしても」の意味にしたい場合には、**even if** を用いることができます。

② **Even if** you don't like it, you must do it.
「もし好きではないとしても、君はそれをしなければなりません」

文頭に **then** を置くことで、「それなら」や「そうすれば」の意味で前の文に続けることができます。カンマに続けて **and** でつなげることで、似たような意味にすることもできます。

③ Hang in there. **Then** something could change.

④ Hang in there, **and** something could change.
「頑張ってください。そうすれば何かが変わりますから」

「そうしなければ」や「そうしないと」の意味で前の文に続けたい場合には、文頭に **otherwise** を置くことで表現することができます。カンマに続けて **or** でつなげることで、似たような意味にすることもできます。

⑤ You should apologize to her first. **Otherwise**, you will be in trouble.

⑥ You should apologize to her first, **or** you will be in trouble.
「君が先に彼女に謝るべきです。そうしなければ、困ったことになりますよ」

Use the Signal

A 空所に入る表現を a〜c から選びましょう。文頭に来る語も小文字になっています。

1. If (　　), your concert will be successful.
2. (　　) if it rains tomorrow.
3. You should follow the doctor's advice.
　 (　　).

a. otherwise, you may not feel better
b. we will cancel the concert
c. you follow my advice

B (　　) 内の語句をヒントにして、次の日本語を英語で表現しましょう。

1. ハチミツを入れると、紅茶はもっとおいしくなります。
(put / your tea)

_____

2. 明日は雨が降っても、その山に行きたいです。
(even if)

_____

Opinions on the Article

A 記事に対するレンのコメントに合うように、下の表の空所を埋めましょう。

DL 32　CD 32

 Ren I think telling a lie is basically bad. If you tell a lie once, you will have to keep lying so that the first one is not revealed. That leads to more lies. For example, I lied and took a day off from my part-time job to go to a concert. Later, I accidentally told my boss about the concert, and I lied again and said that I heard about it from my friend.

嘘についての考え	嘘をつくことは (¹.　　　　　　　　　) 悪いことだ
理由	一度嘘をつくと、その嘘を隠し通すために別の嘘を (².　　　　　　　) なくてはならず、嘘が増える
具体例	嘘をついてバイトを (³.　　　　　) コンサートに行ったが、後日 (⁴.　　　　　) 上司にそのコンサートの話をしてしまい、友人から聞いた、とまた嘘をついた

B 表の内容と合うように、記事に対するリズのコメントの空所に入る語句を選択肢から選びましょう。

DL 33　CD 33

嘘についての考え	嘘をつくことが受け入れられることもある
理由	嘘が人助けになることがある
具体例	電車で老婦人に席を譲ったが遠慮していたようなので、次の駅で降りると嘘をついた

 Liz I think telling a lie is sometimes (¹.　　　　　　　　). Some lies can help people. One day, I was sitting in a (².　　　　　　　　　) on the train and an old lady came and stood in front of me. I wanted to (³.　　　　　　　) the seat to her, but she seemed hesitant. Therefore, I told her that I would (⁴.　　　　　　) the train at the next station even though it was not true.

acceptable　　get off　　give　　seat

Express Your Opinions

嘘をつくことについて、記事へのコメントを書きましょう。

A 前ページの表にならい、意見をまとめましょう。

嘘についての考え	
理由	
具体例	

B 前ページのコメントにならい、上の表にまとめた内容を英語で書きましょう。

I think telling a lie is (   ).

_____

_____

_____

_____

_____

_____

☑ 使用した表現があればチェックをし、これまでのUnitで学んだ表現を使った場合は最後の□の横に書きましょう。

☐ if   ☐ otherwise
☐ even if   ☐ or
☐ then   ☐
☐ and

C ペアやグループで発表しましょう。

UNIT 9

I think I'm going to call in sick today.

深夜バイトの功罪

反対の主張を受け入れる表現 **[even so]**

Important Expressions

🎧 DL 34　⚫ CD 34

[　]内のアルファベットを並び替えて、下線部の日本語を表す英単語を完成させましょう。

1. 今週は夜勤の**シフト**です。　　　　　　　　　　　　[f h i t]（s ＿ ＿ ＿ ＿）

2. 昨日のイタリア語の授業**を欠席**しました。　　　　　[i s s]（m ＿ ＿ ＿）

3. ここが、その映画で私が一番好きな**部分**です。　　　[a r t]（p ＿ ＿ ＿）

4. 皆が正規の**学校教育**を受けるべきです。　　　[c g h i l n o o]（s ＿ ＿ ＿ ＿ ＿ ＿ ＿ ＿）

5. **教育**は、全ての人に対して無償であるべきです。[a c d i n o t u]（e ＿ ＿ ＿ ＿ ＿ ＿ ＿ ＿）

Signal Check

　で囲まれている日本語に対応する英語に○をつけましょう。

1. The store is convenient. Even so, I go there only a few times a year.

   その店は便利です。 そうだとしても 、私は年に数回しかそこへ行きません。

2. Even though your English is not so good, you can have plenty of fun traveling abroad.

   英語があまり上手くない としても 、海外旅行は十分楽しめますよ。

3. It may be true that he has a dirty mouth, but he is a good person.

   口が悪いのは確か かもしれませんが 、彼は良い人です。

Today's Article

次の SNS の投稿を読みましょう。

反対の主張を受け入れる表現に注意して読もう！

@Daiskate wrote:

Of course, like many other students, I need money for school and hanging out with friends. However, I don't want to work for long hours and low pay, so I started working late shifts at a karaoke bar. The pay is high, and I don't have to work weekends. Even so, I already hate it. The hours are very late, so I only get about five hours of sleep before I have to go to school. I'm always sleepy in class, and sometimes I even oversleep and miss classes altogether. Even though I'm making good money, my grades are suffering and I'm so tired every day. I just don't have the energy. I don't want to go to work anymore!

　　　　　2:23 p.m. October 27, 2023

@SoSoSora replied:

Good pay and free weekends? Lucky! I work at a café on Saturdays and Sundays. At first, I thought this was wonderful. Of course, the pay isn't as high as some other jobs, but I wanted to have enough time on school days to finish my assignments and get good sleep every night. So far, that part has been fine. Working on weekends may be great for my schooling, but it's terrible for my social life! My friends are always doing fun things on weekends, and I always have to work! Yes, I'm a student, so my education is the most important thing. But, even so, I want to enjoy my university life, too! I want my weekends back! (>.<)

　　　　　3:15 p.m. October 27, 2023

Notes

altogether「完全に」　make good money「お金をかなり稼ぐ」　suffer「(成績などが) 悪化する」
so far「今のところ」

Take in the Article

A Today's Articleの内容と合うように、空所に適切な日本語を書き入れましょう。

	給料	週末の勤務
カラオケ店でのバイト	(1.　　　　)	(2.　　　)
カフェでのバイト	他の仕事ほど (3.　　　　　)	(4.　　　)

B Today's Articleの内容と合っていればT、そうでなければFを選びましょう。また、問3では、Today's Articleの内容に関するTF問題を英語で作り、ペアで問題を出しあいましょう。

1. @Daiskate wants to continue to work part-time at a karaoke bar.　　　[T / F]

2. @SoSoSora doesn't like her part-time job because she can't hang out with friends on weekends.　　　[T / F]

3. _____ [T / F]

C Today's Articleの内容と合うように、次の質問に英語で答えましょう。また、問3では、Today's Articleの内容に関する質問とその答えを英語で作り、ペアで問題を出しあいましょう。

1. Q How many hours does @Daiskate usually sleep on weekdays?

   A _____

2. Q How does @SoSoSora feel about her job's effect on her sleep schedule?

   A _____

3. Q _____

   A _____

Focus on the Signal

「そうだとしても」というように、ある主張を受け入れつつ反対の意見を述べる場合には、**even so** を用いることができます。even so は普通、文頭で用います。

① Many people say this fashion is outdated. **Even so**, I love it.
　　「このファッションは時代遅れだという人が多いです。**そうだとしても**、私はそれが大好きです」

even so に似た表現に、Unit 3 で学習した **even though** があります。ただし、even so は①、even though は②のように使い方が異なります。

② **Even though** her story makes sense, no one believes her.
　　「彼女の話は辻褄が合っている**としても**、誰も信じていません」

ある主張を受け入れる表現として、**It may be ○○ that ..., but ~.**「…であることは○○かもしれないが、～」がよく用いられます。○○には **true**、**certain**、**great** などが入ります。…で相手の意見を、～で自分の意見を述べます。

③ **It may be** true **that** your idea is economical, **but** my idea would be more effective.
　　「君の考えが経済的**なのは**確か**かもしれませんが**、私のアイデアの方が効果的でしょう」

また、④のように、**of course**「もちろん」という表現を用いた後で、**but** や **however** などの逆接の表現を重ねることで、同様の意味にすることができます。

④ **Of course**, he is talented. **However**, he succeeded thanks to his hard work.
　　「**もちろん**、彼には才能があります。**しかし**、成功したのは努力のおかげです」

Use the Signal

A 空所に入る表現を a ～ c から選びましょう。文頭に来る語も小文字になっています。

1. Your teaching is good. Even so, (　　). 　　**a.** I'm nineteen
2. Even though (　　), I love music from 　　**b.** he kept dancing
　 the 1980s. 　　**c.** this musical instrument
3. (　　) even though the music stopped. 　　　 is difficult for me

B (　　) 内の語句をヒントにして、次の日本語を英語で表現しましょう。

1. She has the right to know the truth. そうだとしても、私はそれを言いたくありません。

　　_____

2. 私たちが勝つ見込みがないのは確かかもしれませんが、やってみるべきです。
　 (have no chance)

　　_____

Opinions on the Article

A 投稿に対するトムの返答に合うように、下の表の空所を埋めましょう。

DL 36 CD 36

@Tom replied: I think working during the day on weekends is better than working until late at night on weekdays. Of course, we need money to enjoy our university life. Even so, our health is the most important. You have to balance learning, working, and sleeping. Even though the pay rates for daytime jobs are not always high, there are some jobs which pay well, such as a cram school teacher or a private tutor.

アルバイトについての考え	平日に深夜まで働くよりも (¹.　　　　　　) に働くほうがよい
理由1	健康が最も大切。学習と仕事と睡眠の (².　　　　) を取る必要がある
理由2	(³.　　) の講師や (⁴.　　　　　) など、昼の仕事で給料が高いものもある

B 表の内容と合うように、投稿に対するミオの返答の空所に入る語を選択肢から選びましょう。

DL 37 CD 37

アルバイトについての考え	週末の昼に働くより、平日に深夜まで働く方がよい
理由1	夜間の仕事なら短い時間で多くの給料をもらえる
理由2	スケジュールを上手く管理して、仕事前に昼寝をすれば、睡眠時間も問題ない

@Mio replied: I think working until late at night on (¹.　　　　　) is better than working during the day on (².　　　　　). As they say, "Time is money." I think it's better if I work for a (³.　　　　) time and earn a lot of money. Night jobs, such as convenience store clerks and karaoke bar staff, make this possible. Also, if you (⁴.　　　　　) your schedule well and take a nap before work, you will have no problem with your amount of sleep.

manage　　short　　weekdays　　weekends

Express Your Opinions

大学生のアルバイトについて、投稿への返答を書きましょう。

A 前ページの表にならい、意見をまとめましょう。

アルバイトについての考え	
理由	

B 前ページのコメントにならい、上の表にまとめた内容を英語で書きましょう。

I think (   )

is better than (   ).

_____

_____

_____

_____

_____

☑ 使用した表現があればチェックをし、これまでのUnitで学んだ表現を使った場合は最後の□の横に書きましょう。

☐ even so
☐ even though
☐ It may be true [certain, great]
  that ..., but ~.

☐ Of course ..., but ~.
☐ Of course .... However, ~.
☐

C ペアやグループで発表しましょう。

They are open twenty-four-seven!

コンビニの在り方改革

 具体的な情報をつけ加える表現（1） **[such as]**

Important Expressions

🎧 DL 38 ◎ CD 38

[　　] 内のアルファベットを並び替えて、下線部の日本語を表す英単語を完成させましょう。

1. あなたは**追加の**20ドルが必要です。　　　　[a d d i i l n o t]（a _ _ _ _ _ _ _ _ _）

2. この階のどの部屋も**利用可能**です。　　　　[a a b e i l l v]（a _ _ _ _ _ _ _ _）

3. 私のスーツケース**を引きずら**ないでください。　　　　[a g r]（d _ _ _）

4. **(公共)料金**の支払いを忘れました。　　　　[l l i]（b _ _ _）

5. 彼は両親に**頼り**すぎです。　　　　[e l y]（r _ _ _）

Signal Check

　で囲まれている日本語に対応する英語に○をつけましょう。

1. I want to get a job related to children, such as a nursery school teacher.

例えば 保育士 のような 、子どもと関わる仕事がしたいです。

2. I love driving along ocean roads, like the Great Ocean Road.

例えば グレート・オーシャン・ロード のような 、海沿いの道路をドライブするのが好きです。

3. Finally, if you like, you can add mayonnaise, mustard, and so on.

最後に、お好みに応じて、マヨネーズやマスタード など を加えてください。

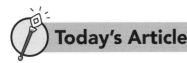

Today's Article

DL 39　CD 39

次の記事を読みましょう。

具体的な情報をつけ加える表現に注意して読もう！

By Aiden Scott

November 29, 2023 at 1:00 p.m.

As a foreigner living in Japan, I'm surprised by something new almost every day. Japan is full of things that I've never seen in my home country, like public transportation that is always on time or good service at fast food restaurants. Recently, I learned about convenience stores in Japan. Of course, if you need a snack or a drink when you are out, they have sodas, chips, sandwiches, and so on. They also have many things you might need at home, including medicine and toilet paper. However, I was really surprised by the additional services that are available! Here is one example. When you are about to travel somewhere but don't want to drag your heavy suitcase with you, you can ship it to your destination from any convenience store! Many people also go to convenience stores to pay bills, such as electricity or water, too! You can even buy tickets for concerts or amusement parks there! These stores are really impressive!

However, is it possible that Japanese convenience stores are actually too convenient? I mean, it's great that they are open 24 hours a day, but is that really necessary? How many people actually go there at 3 a.m.? Also, there are too many of them! They are on almost every corner, and sometimes, you can find two right next to each other! I'm worried that I already rely too much on them. This week, I bought all of my food there instead of cooking at home. That's probably not good for my health or my wallet. Am I the only one with this problem?

Notes

public transportation「公共交通機関」
on time「時間通りに」
be about to ~「(まさに) ~しようとしている」
destination「目的地」

Take in the Article

A Today's Articleの内容と合うように、空所に適切な日本語を書き入れましょう。

コンビニの利点	・外出時に (**1.**) や飲み物を買える 　→ (**具体例**) 炭酸飲料、ポテトチップス、(**2.**) ・自宅で必要な物を買える 　→ (**具体例**) (**3.**)、トイレットペーパー ・物を買う以外のサービス 　→ (**具体例**) 荷物の発送、(**4.**) の支払い、チケットの購入
コンビニの問題点	・24時間営業の必要性 ・店の数が多すぎる

B Today's Articleの内容と合っていればT、そうでなければFを選びましょう。また、問3では、Today's Articleの内容に関するTF問題を英語で作り、ペアで問題を出しあいましょう。

1. You can buy anything, such as a suitcase, in a convenience store. 　　[T / F]

2. The writer wonders if convenience stores should be open 24 hours a day. 　[T / F]

3. _____ [T / F]

C Today's Articleの内容と合うように、次の質問に英語で答えましょう。また、問3では、Today's Articleの内容に関する質問とその答えを英語で作り、ペアで問題を出しあいましょう。

1. **Q** Has the writer known about Japanese convenience stores for a long time?

　A _____

2. **Q** Why doesn't the writer think it's good to buy his food at a convenience store?

　A _____

3. **Q** _____

　A _____

Focus on the Signal

「(例えば) ～のような」のように、具体例をつけ加える場合には、**such as** を用いることができます。such as の後ろには、名詞を置くことが多いです。

① I don't like spicy sauces, **such as** chili sauce and Tabasco.
「チリソースやタバスコ**のような**、辛いソースが苦手です」

such as の他に、**like** や **including** を用いることもできます。②のように **for example** を用いることもできます。また、**say** を用いることもできますが、前後でカンマを付けて用いるのが普通です（③）。like や including は①のように、後ろにカンマを付けません。

② You'll look fashionable if you match the colors of accessories, **for example**, socks and a scarf.
「小物、**例えば**靴下とスカーフとか、の色を合わせると、おしゃれに見えますよ」

③ Some states in America, **say** California and Texas, are bigger than Japan.
「いくつかのアメリカの州、**例えば**カリフォルニアやテキサスは、日本より大きいです」

「～など」と言いたい場合には、具体例の後で **and so on** を付けることで表現することができます。

④ In this area, we can see goats, sheep, rabbits, **and so on.**
「このエリアでは、ヤギや羊、ウサギ**など**を見ることができます」

Use the Signal

A 空所に入る表現を a～c から選びましょう。

1. I'm not fond of insects, such as (　　).
2. I read various kinds of novels, such as (　　).
3. I've had some part-time jobs, such as (　　).

a. serving customers and cleaning
b. mosquitoes and bees
c. mysteries and science fiction

B (　　) 内の語句をヒントにして、次の日本語を英語で表現しましょう。

1. 私はテトリスのような、単純なゲームが好きです。
(simple / such as / Tetris)

_____

2. この店では、バスオイルや入浴剤などを扱っています。
(sells / bath oils / bath bombs / and so on)

_____

Opinions on the Article

A 記事に対するレンのコメントに合うように、下の表の空所を埋めましょう。

DL 40　CD 40

Ren
I don't think convenience stores are too convenient. Opening 24/7 is especially important to me. For example, I can buy meals after I finish my part-time job at midnight. When I play baseball early in the morning, I can buy my favorite drinks. They are worthwhile because they are open when the other stores aren't. They are definitely necessary for people working at night, such as truck drivers and road construction crews.

主張	コンビニは便利すぎるとは思わない
理由	毎日（ **1.** 　　　　　　） 開いているということが重要
具体的なエピソード	・夜中や（ **2.** 　　　　　） に飲食物を買うことができる ・トラック運転手や（ **3.** 　　　　　　　　　　） など、 　夜間に働く人にとって（ **4.** 　　　　　　）

B 表の内容と合うように、記事に対するリズのコメントの空所に入る語を選択肢から選びましょう。

DL 41　CD 41

主張	コンビニは便利すぎる
理由	数が多すぎる
具体的なエピソード	・コンビニは多くの在庫を準備しがちであるため、毎日大量の食品が賞味期限切れになり、廃棄されなければならない ・人手不足によるスタッフの長時間労働が起こりやすい

Liz
I think convenience stores are too convenient. There are (**1.** 　　　　　) many of them. The stores tend to (**2.** 　　　　　) too many groceries, including food and drinks. A lot of those (**3.** 　　　　　) and must be thrown out every day. Also, I hear many stores are facing staff (**4.** 　　　　　). Each staff member will have to work long hours in order to keep the stores open 24 hours a day.

expire　shortages　stock　too

Express Your Opinions

コンビニの在り方について、記事へのコメントを書きましょう。

A 前ページの表にならい、意見をまとめましょう。

主張	
理由	
具体的なエピソード	

B 前ページのコメントにならい、上の表にまとめた内容を英語で書きましょう。

I (   ) convenience stores are too convenient. _____

_____

_____

_____

_____

_____

☑ 使用した表現があればチェックをし、これまでのUnitで学んだ表現を使った場合は最後の□の横に書きましょう。

☐ such as   ☐ say
☐ like   ☐ and so on
☐ for example   ☐
☐ including

C ペアやグループで発表しましょう。

It was the best four years of my life.

身が入らないときは

具体的な情報をつけ加える表現（2）　**[for example]**

Important Expressions

🎧 DL 42　💿 CD 42

[　　]内のアルファベットを並び替えて、下線部の日本語を表す英単語を完成させましょう。

1. やる気を持ち続けるのは難しいです。　　　　　　　[a d e i o t t v]（m _ _ _ _ _ _ _ _ ）

2. リンダはとても身の回りが整理されているので、プリントを失くしません。

　　　　　　　　　　　　　　　　　　　　　[a d e g i n r z]（o _ _ _ _ _ _ _ _ ）

3. 締切はすでに過ぎました。　　　　　　　　　　　[a d e e i l n]（d _ _ _ _ _ _ _ ）

4. それはストレスを軽減するのに役立ちます。　　　　[e e e i l v]（r _ _ _ _ _ _ ）

5. ネットニュースを読むのが私の日課です。　　　　　　[e i n o t u]（r _ _ _ _ _ _ ）

Signal Check

□で囲まれている日本語に対応する英語に〇をつけましょう。

1. You should use your mornings more wisely. For example, try to do 15-minute stretches.

あなたは朝をもっと有意義に使うべきです。例えば、15分のストレッチをしてみましょう。

2. Every dish is delicious in this restaurant. For instance, the quiche is exceptional!

このレストランの料理はどれもおいしいです。例えば、キッシュは格別です！

3. Suppose you are taking the train home now.

今、帰りの電車に乗っていると仮定してみましょう。

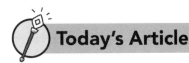

Today's Article

次の記事を読みましょう。

 具体的な情報をつけ加える表現に注意して読もう！

 By Janet Bloomer
January 5, 2024 at 3:00 p.m.

Many people say that university was the best four years of their lives. However, some people find it stressful and difficult. If you want to be one of the people who enjoys university life, you have to stay motivated. Here are a few tips to help you do that.

Classes are more fun when you're motivated, but it is easy to lose motivation when the classwork feels difficult. Being organized can help. For example, write your notes in a notebook instead of on random papers. Similarly, keep your handouts in files so that they don't get lost. This way, everything you need to know is all in one place.

Managing your schedule is the next step. Suppose you have a teacher that often gives homework or tests. You should write those test dates and deadlines in a calendar. Also, make a study schedule for yourself. If you do homework and study a little every day, you won't have to rush and feel stressed out the night before.

Getting good grades is important, but having fun in university is too! Find ways to make friends and have fun to help you relieve stress. For instance, try to join a club or circle. They are great for meeting new people and making memories. If you hear about interesting events on campus, attend those, too! Without having fun, it is easy to feel burned out from classwork.

University life is great when you have a balanced routine for your studies and your social life. Stay organized, manage your schedule, and make time for fun, too. This way, you will enjoy coming to campus every day.

Notes

stressed out「ストレス疲れする」
burned out「燃え尽きる」

Take in the Article

A Today's Articleの内容と合うように、空所に適切な日本語を書き入れましょう。

	1つ目	2つ目	3つ目
やる気を保つヒント	身の回りを整理する	スケジュールを管理する	大学生活を楽しむ
具体例	・授業中のメモを（^{1.}　　　　　　）に取る ・配布資料をファイルにまとめる	・（^{2.}　　　　　　）や（^{3.}　　　　　　）をカレンダーに書く ・学習の予定を立てる	・（^{4.}　　　　　　）やサークルに入る ・興味のあるイベントに参加する

B Today's Articleの内容と合っていればT、そうでなければFを選びましょう。また、問3では、Today's Articleの内容に関するTF問題を英語で作り、ペアで問題を出しあいましょう。

1. Making a study schedule is one way to keep motivated.　　　　　　[T / F]

2. Having fun is as important as getting good grades in university.　　　[T / F]

3. _____[T / F]

C Today's Articleの内容と合うように、次の質問に英語で答えましょう。また、問3では、Today's Articleの内容に関する質問とその答えを英語で作り、ペアで問題を出しあいましょう。

1. **Q** What is an advantage of keeping your handouts in files?

   A _____

2. **Q** What are you likely to feel if you don't study a little every day?

   A _____

3. **Q** _____

   A _____

Focus on the Signal

前の文に続けて具体例にあたる文を書く場合には、**for example** や **for instance** を用いることができます。これらの表現は文頭に置くことが普通ですが、文中や文末に置くこともできます。

① His songs are all famous. **For example**, his debut single sold a million copies.

② His songs are all famous. His debut single sold a million copies, **for instance**.

「彼の歌はどれも有名です。**例えば**、デビューシングルはミリオンセラーになりました」

「～ということを仮定［想定］してみましょう」というように、具体例を示したい場合には、文頭に **Suppose** を置くことで表現できます。

③ Having a driver's license can help with your job hunt. **Suppose** you find a job offer that requires driving to different cities. With a license, you will have an advantage over others.

「運転免許を持っていると、就職に役立ちます。別の都市へ運転する必要がある仕事の募集がある**と仮定してみましょう**。免許があれば、他の人よりも有利です」

Use the Signal

A 空所に入る表現を a ～ c から選びましょう。

1. This studio can be used for many things. For example, (　　　).

2. Cow eyes are different from human eyes in many ways. For example, (　　　).

3. There are many means of transportation. For example, (　　　).

a. the former are oval and the latter are round

b. you can practice yoga here

c. it takes 20 minutes by bus

B (　　) 内の語句をヒントにして、次の日本語を英語で表現しましょう。

1. Many animals can run much faster than humans. 例えば、トナカイは人間のおよそ2倍の速さで走ることができます。

(reindeer / twice as fast as)

_____

2. 君がそれをすると仮定してみましょう。

(suppose)

_____

Opinions on the Article

A 記事に対するトムのコメントに合うように、下の表の空所を埋めましょう。

DL 44　CD 44

Tom

I think the key to a successful university life is having friends. Good friends are not only for hanging out with but will help you in many situations. For example, when a teacher gives you a tough assignment, you can help each other. When you are worrying about your future, they will listen to you. Many lifelong friendships start in university.

大切なこと・もの	友人
理由	良い友人は一緒に (**1.**　　　　　　　　　　) だけでなく、さまざまな場面で助けてくれる
具体例	・難しい (**2.**　　　　　) が出たときに (**3.**　　　　　　　) ことができる ・将来について (**4.**　　　　　　) いるとき、話を聞いてくれる

B 表の内容と合うように、記事に対するミオのコメントの空所に入る語句を選択肢から選びましょう。　DL 45　CD 45

大切なこと・もの	大学の外での社会的な活動
理由	社会的な活動からの学びは大学での学びとは異なる
具体例	・アルバイトは社会人として働くことを学ぶ良い機会になる ・ボランティア活動に参加すると、社会問題について多く学べる

Mio

I think the key to a successful university life is engaging in (**1.**　　　　　　　　　) outside the university. You can learn different things from these activities than you can at university. For instance, part-time jobs offer many (**2.**　　　　　　　　) for you to know what working as a member of (**3.**　　　　　　　　) is like. Also, if you do volunteer work, you can learn a lot about (**4.**　　　　　　　　). Don't limit yourself to just the campus. Try various things!

opportunities　　society　　social activities　　social issues

Unit 11 ▪ It was the best four years of my life.　73

Express Your Opinions

良い大学生活を送る秘訣について、記事へのコメントを書きましょう。

A 前ページの表にならい、意見をまとめましょう。

大切なこと・もの	
理由	
具体例	

B 前ページのコメントにならい、上の表にまとめた内容を英語で書きましょう。

I think the key to a successful university life is （

）. _____

_____

_____

_____

_____

_____

☑ 使用した表現があればチェックをし、これまでのUnitで学んだ表現を使った場合は最後の□の横に書きましょう。

☐ for example   ☐ suppose

☐ for instance   ☐

C ペアやグループで発表しましょう。

UNIT 12

... but can it make an omelet?

スマホで十分？

2つのことを比べる表現　[while]

Important Expressions

🎧 DL 46　💿 CD 46

[　]内のアルファベットを並び替えて、下線部の日本語を表す英単語を完成させましょう。

1. あなたの帽子は、私のものと**比較すると**小さいです。

[a d e m o p r] (c _ _ _ _ _ _ _)

2. 彼がしたことは**信じられないほど**勇敢です。　[b c d e i l n r y] (i _ _ _ _ _ _ _ _)

3. 私の方にカメラを**向け**ないでください。　[i n o t] (p _ _ _ _)

4. そんな**小さな**家には住みたくありません。　[i n y] (t _ _ _)

5. **支払**方法はどうなさいますか。　[a e m n t y] (p _ _ _ _ _ _)

Signal Check

　　　で囲まれている日本語に対応する英語に○をつけましょう。

1. I usually eat it with a fork, while my brother eats it with chopsticks.

私は普段それをフォークで食べますが、一方で弟は箸で食べます。

2. Whereas I used to watch TV to get information 10 years ago, I tend to use my smartphone now.

私は10年前にはテレビで情報を得ていた一方で、今はスマホを用いることが多いです。

3. He is shocked at the result. In contrast, she looks happy.

彼はその結果にショックを受けています。対照的に、彼女は幸せそうです。

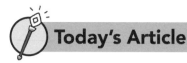

Today's Article

DL 47   CD 47

次のブログを読みましょう。

2つのことを比べる表現に注意して読もう！

My son's phone
January 24, 2024 at 4:45 p.m.

When I was a kid, my dad often told me stories about his childhood. He used to say, "back in my day …" and then tell me how difficult his life was compared to mine. "Technology has made everything so convenient for you kids," he would say. Now, I find myself feeling the same way about my son and his smartphone. I wish I had had one of those when I was his age. They're incredibly convenient!

I usually had to flip through a dictionary to look up words I didn't know, while my son can do that almost instantly on his phone. I remember that studying foreign languages was especially tough. Meanwhile, I see my son just pointing his phone's camera at his books and getting full translations. As you know, smartphones can do more than that, too. My son can listen to literally any song he can think of on his phone. In contrast, I used to have a large collection of CDs, and I could only carry a few discs with me at one time. Even the way we enjoy videos is different. Whereas watching movies on TV used to be a family experience, my son enjoys watching them alone on that tiny screen. He talks to all of his friends on it, he makes payments on it, and he somehow even goes sightseeing on it! I wouldn't be surprised if it made breakfast for him, too!

It makes everything so easy for him. That is why I wonder if it's actually *too* convenient. I mean, because my son relies on it for everything, can he do anything without it?

Notes

flip through ~「〜をぱらぱらめくる」
look up ~「〜を調べる」
literally「文字どおりに」
somehow「何らかの形で」

Take in the Article

A Today's Articleの内容と合うように、空所に適切な日本語を書き入れましょう。

	子どものころの筆者	筆者の息子
単語を調べる	(1.　　　　　　　　　) を用いた	(2.　　　　　　　　　) を用いる
音楽を聴く	(3.　　　　　) で聴いた	(4.　　　　　) で聴く
家で映画を見る	(5.　　　　　　　) で家族と見た	(6.　　　　　　　) で一人で見る

B Today's Articleの内容と合っていればT、そうでなければFを選びましょう。また、問3では、Today's Articleの内容に関するTF問題を英語で作り、ペアで問題を出しあいましょう。

1. The writer carried many CDs with her when she went out. [T / F]

2. The writer's son enjoys sightseeing without leaving home. [T / F]

3. _____ [T / F]

C Today's Articleの内容と合うように、次の質問に英語で答えましょう。また、問3では、Today's Articleの内容に関する質問とその答えを英語で作り、ペアで問題を出しあいましょう。

1. Q What kind of stories did the writer's father often tell her when she was a kid?

A _____

2. Q With whom does the writer's son usually enjoy watching movies?

A _____

3. Q _____

A _____

Focus on the Signal

1つの文の中で、「その一方で」のように2つのことを比較したい場合には、**while** や **whereas** で文と文をつなげて表現することができます。while や whereas は文頭にも文中にも置くことができます。

① I like your idea, **while** he might not agree with it.

② **While** I like your idea, he might not agree with it.

「私は君の考えが好きだけれど、**その一方で**彼は同意しないかもしれません」

前の文と比較する形で、「その一方で」「対照的に」のようにもう1つのことを続けて言いたい場合には、**meanwhile**、**on the other hand**、**in contrast**、**in comparison** などを用いることができます。これらの表現は文頭に置くことが普通ですが、カンマを用いて文中に置くことも可能です。

③ The birth rate in this country is increasing. **In contrast**, mortality remains low.

「この国の出生率は上がっています。**対照的に**、死亡率は低いままです」

④ I've read this novel six times. She, **on the other hand**, didn't even buy it.

「私はこの小説を6回読みました。**一方**、彼女は買ってさえいません」

Use the Signal

A 空所に入る表現を a ~ c から選びましょう。

1. Everything I said is true, while (   ).

2. While (   ), only two people chose the other one.

3. I gave a brooch to my mother. On the other hand, (   ).

a. my father bought her a scarf

b. many people joined her seminar

c. she made everything up

B (   ) 内の語句をヒントにして、次の日本語を英語で表現しましょう。

1. 私は日本史に興味がありますが、一方で姉はイギリスの歴史に興味があります。

(Japanese history / while / British history)

_____

2. My girlfriend doesn't eat meat.その一方で、私はハンバーガーなしの生活は考えられません。

(imagine / without hamburgers)

_____

Opinions on the Article

A ブログに対するレンのコメントに合うように、下の表の空所を埋めましょう。

DL 48　　CD 48

We should make the best use of smartphones. Some people say that we rely too much on them. However, smartphones didn't change what we do but how we do it. For example, 20 years ago, if we wanted to read books, take photographs, and buy drinks at the park, we needed to carry books, cameras, and wallets with us. In contrast, people today don't need to carry much at all. They can do all of that and more with their smartphones. We can stay mobile with them.

主張	スマホを (¹.　　　　　　　) に活用すべき
理由	スマホが変えたのは私たちが (².　　　　　　　　　) ではなく、 (³.　　　　　　　　) だ
具体例	20年前には本、カメラ、財布を持ち歩かなければならなかったが、今はスマホさえあればそれら全てのことができ、(⁴.　　　　　) でいられる

B 表の内容と合うように、ブログに対するリズのコメントの空所に入る語を選択肢から選びましょう。

DL 49　　CD 49

主張	スマホに頼りすぎるべきではない
理由	スマホで全てのことができるわけではないので、スマホ以外の機器も使えるようになるべき
具体例	友人はフリック入力は上手いが、キーボードでの入力は上手にできず、パソコンで卒業論文を書く際に苦労している

We should not (¹.　　　　　　) on smartphones too much. We can do many things with them, but not everything. This is why you should be able to use other (².　　　　　　) as well. For instance, one of my friends is very good at flick (³.　　　　　　) on smartphones, while she cannot type on a keyboard well. Because of this, she is having a hard time writing her graduation (⁴.　　　　　) on her computer.

devices　　rely　　thesis　　typing

Express Your Opinions

スマホについて、ブログへのコメントを書きましょう。

A 前ページの表にならい、意見をまとめましょう。

主張	
理由	
具体例	

B 前ページのコメントにならい、上の表にまとめた内容を英語で書きましょう。

We should (　　　　　　　　　　　　　　　　　　　　　　　　　　).

_____

_____

_____

_____

_____

☑ 使用した表現があればチェックをし、これまでのUnitで学んだ表現を使った場合は最後の□の横に書きましょう。

☐ while　　　　　　　　　　　☐ in contrast
☐ whereas　　　　　　　　　　☐ in comparison
☐ meanwhile　　　　　　　　　☐
☐ on the other hand

C ペアやグループで発表しましょう。

UNIT 13

It's my new best friend.

私のトモダチ

自分の言いたいことを強める表現　**[in my opinion]**

Important Expressions

🎧 DL 50　💿 CD 50

[　]内のアルファベットを並び替えて、下線部の日本語を表す英単語を完成させましょう。

1. それがどこにあるか案内しますよ。私<u>についてきて</u>ください。　[l l o o w]（f _ _ _ _ _ ）

2. この新しいロボットは、6つの異なる<u>感情</u>を表すことができます。

[i m n o o t]（e _ _ _ _ _ _ ）

3. 運転中はいつもガム<u>を噛み</u>ます。　　　　　　　　[e h w]（c _ _ _ ）

4. 何か<u>変な</u>ことが起こっていると思います。　　　[a l n s u u]（u _ _ _ _ _ _ ）

5. 今<u>すぐに</u>伺います。　　　　　　　　　　　　　[g h i t]（r _ _ _ _ ）

Signal Check

☐ で囲まれている日本語に対応する英語に〇をつけましょう。

1. You can use a bus or a train. In my opinion, it's better to take a bus.

バスか電車を使うことができます。 | 個人的には | 、バスで行った方がよい | と思います | 。

2. I didn't enjoy the date with him. In fact, I don't like zoos so much.

彼とのデートは楽しめませんでした。 | 実を言うと | 、動物園はあまり好きではありません。

3. Many things can make you sick while abroad. Above all, be careful about what you eat.

海外での体調不良の原因はたくさんあります。 | とりわけ | 、口にするものには注意してください。

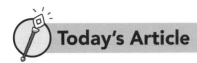

Today's Article

次の広告を読みましょう。

> 自分の言いたいことを強める表現に注意して読もう！

Your New Best Friend
Robo-Pet

Do you wish you had a pet but live in an apartment that doesn't allow them? Are you worried that having a pet is a big responsibility? Well, worry no more! Introducing Robo-Pet, from Pet-Tech! This cute robotic animal is the little friend you've always wanted, without all the hassles of owning a cat or dog. Thanks to its advanced A.I., Robo-Pet can do everything normal pets do, and more! It listens to voice commands, follows you around when you walk, and even plays fetch! It shows emotions, too! In dog mode, it wags its tail and barks when excited, and in cat mode, it purrs and meows!

"I think he's a lot of fun! I can go walking with him in the morning, so exercising is more fun now. He's even good at catching balls in the air when I throw them. Robo-Pet can be really helpful, too. He wakes me up for work or sets timers for me when I'm cooking. Above all, Robo-Pet is my friend!　　　　　　　　　　　　　　　　　　(Tiffany, New York, 23)

"It's like having a pet with no stress. I mean, it doesn't rip up my furniture or chew my shoes, and it doesn't need to poop! In fact, I feel much safer when I leave him at home. With 'patrol mode,' it walks around the house and sends pictures and messages to my phone if it sees or hears anything unusual. In my opinion, it's better than a real dog!"　　　　　　　　　　　　　　　　　　　　(John, Osaka, 42)

Order your Robo-Pet online today, and get free delivery right to your door!

Notes

hassle「面倒なこと」　play fetch「物を投げて、動物にそれを取りに行かせる遊びをする」
wag「（しっぽなど）を振る」　bark「吠える」　purr「（猫が）のどを鳴らす」　meow「ニャオと鳴く」
rip up ~「～をズタズタに引き裂く」　poop「うんちをする」

Take in the Article

A Today's Articleの内容と合うように、空所に適切な日本語を書き入れましょう。

	ロボペットの良さ	ロボペットが役立つ点
ティファニー	(1.　　　　　) やキャッチボールができる	(2.　　　　　　　　　) やタイマーの代わりになる
ジョン	・(3.　　　　　) や靴にいたずらをしない ・トイレが必要ない	(4.　　　　　　　　　) を感知すると知らせてくれる

B Today's Articleの内容と合っていればT、そうでなければFを選びましょう。また、問3では、Today's Articleの内容に関するTF問題を英語で作り、ペアで問題を出しあいましょう。

1. If you want both a robo-dog and a robo-cat, you must buy two Robo-Pets.　[T / F]

2. You might not want to leave your shoes near your Robo-Pet.　　　　　[T / F]

3. _____　[T / F]

C Today's Articleの内容と合うように、次の質問に英語で答えましょう。また、問3では、Today's Articleの内容に関する質問とその答えを英語で作り、ペアで問題を出しあいましょう。

1. **Q** Who talks about the functions of the Robo-Pet that real pets can't do, Tiffany, John, or both?

   A _____

2. **Q** How much will the delivery fee be if you buy a Robo-Pet online today?

   A _____

3. **Q** _____

   A _____

Focus on the Signal

自分の主張や要点を強める表現に、**in my opinion**、**actually**、**indeed**、**clearly**、**in fact**、**after all**、**above all**、**I mean** などがあります。これらの表現を用いなくても文法的に正しい文章を書くことはできますが、用いることでより効果的に自分の主張を読み手・聞き手に伝えることができます。文中で用いることができるものもありますが、文頭で用いる場合が多いです。

① **In my opinion,** Jessica would make a better leader than Jack. She is more responsible.

「**個人的には**、ジェシカの方が、ジャックよりも良い指導者になる**と思います**。彼女の方が、より責任感がありますから」

② His explanation was difficult. **Actually,** I couldn't understand what he said at all.

「彼の説明は難しかったです。**実のところ**、彼の言っていることは何も分かりませんでした」

日本語の「〜と思います」や「個人的には」といったニュアンスで、I think を用いることがよくあります。しかし、I think ばかりを多用すると不自然な英文になってしまうため、上記のような類似表現のバリエーションを覚えておくとよいでしょう。

Use the Signal

A 空所に入る表現を a ~ c から選びましょう。

1. You say the cap looks good on me.
   In my opinion, (　　　).

2. I don't think we need a toaster.
   In fact, (　　　).

3. My boss is friendly to everyone.
   I mean, (　　　).

a. it doesn't really suit me

b. I always see him smile

c. I rarely buy white bread

B (　　　) 内の語句をヒントにして、次の日本語を英語で表現しましょう。

1. 個人的には、彼は謝るべきだと思います。
   (opinion / apologize)

   _____

2. 何よりもまず、体調に気を付けてください。（ご自愛ください。）
   (above / take good care of)

   _____

Opinions on the Article

A 広告を読んだトムの感想に合うように、下の表の空所を埋めましょう。

DL 52　CD 52

 Tom

I prefer having a Robo-Pet to having real pets. This is because a Robo-Pet is so much easier to take care of. I don't have to feed it or brush it. When I go on a trip, it's even possible to switch it off. Also, I don't have to worry about its health. Robo-Pets don't get sick. Above all, I can have a lot of fun with it, and it can help me on many occasions. If I own one, it will definitely be my real buddy!

どんなペットを好むか	(1.　　　　　　　　　　　　)
理由	ロボペットは実際のペットと比べてはるかに (2.　　　　　　)
具体例	・(3.　　　　　　　　　　　) 必要もブラシをかける必要もない ・旅行に行くときは (4.　　　　　　　　) ことさえできる ・健康を心配しなくてよい

B 表の内容と合うように、広告を読んだミオの感想の空所に入る語を選択肢から選びましょう。

DL 53　CD 53

どんなペットを好むか	本物のペット
理由	本物のペットを飼うことは、かけがえのない経験をもたらす
具体例	10年間飼っている犬と一緒に裏庭で遊んだり、一緒にお風呂に入ったり、一緒に寝たりしたことは全て良い思い出

Mio

I prefer having (1.　　　　　　　　) pets to having a Robo-Pet. This is because we can have (2.　　　　　　　　) experiences with them. I have had a dog for 10 years. I remember when she first came to my home. I played with her in the (3.　　　　　　　　), I took a bath with her, and I even slept with her. Every one of these is a happy (4.　　　　　　　　) for me. After all, if my pet were a robot, I don't think I could feel like this.

backyard　　memory　　precious　　real

Express Your Opinions

ロボペットに関する広告を読んで、ペットについてのあなたの感想を書きましょう。

A 前ページの表にならい、感想をまとめましょう。

どんなペットを好むか	
理由	
具体例	

B 前ページの感想にならい、上の表にまとめた内容を英語で書きましょう。

I prefer having (　　　　　　　　　　　) to having (　　　　　　　).

_____

_____

_____

_____

_____

✔️ 使用した表現があればチェックをし、これまでのUnitで学んだ表現を使った場合は最後の□の横に書きましょう。

☐ in my opinion　　　　　☐ after all
☐ actually　　　　　　　 ☐ above all
☐ indeed　　　　　　　　☐ I mean
☐ clearly　　　　　　　　☐
☐ in fact

C ペアやグループで発表しましょう。

Stick with what you know?

やりたいこと？　向いていること？

自分の言いたいことを弱める表現　**[may]**

Important Expressions

🎧 DL 54　💿 CD 54

[　]内のアルファベットを並び替えて、下線部の日本語を表す英単語を完成させましょう。

1. 私はこの会社に<u>応募し</u>ています。　　　　　　　　　　[l p p y]（a _ _ _ _）

2. 私は15日に就職の<u>面接</u>があります。　　　　[e e i n r t v w]（i _ _ _ _ _ _ _ _）

3. 私は料理が<u>結構</u>得意です。　　　　　　　　　　[e r t t y]（p _ _ _ _ _）

4. 仕事探しは<u>ストレスが多い</u>です。　　　　　[e f l r s s t u]（s _ _ _ _ _ _ _）

5. これは世界で一番<u>退屈な</u>ゲームかもしれません。　　[g i n o r]（b _ _ _ _ _）

Signal Check

☐で囲まれている日本語に対応する英語に〇をつけましょう。

1. As you may have already heard, I'm going to join this project.

　もう既にご存じ かもしれません が、私はこのプロジェクトに参加します。

2. She probably bought this book just because the cover is beautiful.

　彼女は表紙が綺麗という理由だけでこの本を買ったの かもしれません 。

3. It is likely that we have to pay more.

　私たちはもっとお金を支払わなければならない かもしれません 。

 **Today's Article**

次のブログを読みましょう。

言いたいことを弱める表現に注意して読もう！

 Job hunting
June 12, 2024 at 3:10 p.m.

As most of you probably already know, I have been job hunting for the last few months. Like many other university students, I've applied to maybe a hundred different companies. I even had several interviews, but it seemed like no one wanted to hire me. However, I finally have some good news! I got job offers from two really good companies! One is for a programming job, and the other is for a customer service job.

Now I have a new dilemma: Which job should I choose? To be honest, I'm more interested in the second one. It looks like it would be fun, and it's with a famous company. Unfortunately, customer service means that I will be talking to people every day, but as you may already know, I'm a very shy person. I'm worried that I won't be very good. I'm really not good at speaking with others. On the other hand, with the programming job, it is likely that I won't have to speak to anyone most of the time. Not only that, but I've learned some programming before, and I was actually pretty good at it. The problem here is that many people say programming jobs can be stressful. Also, I would have to sit in front of a computer all day. I might be shy, but I don't know if I want that.

I'm really having trouble deciding. Should I take the job that may be difficult for me but looks fun, or should I settle for the boring job that I will probably be really good at? What should I do?

Notes

job hunting「就職活動」
job offer「内定」
to be honest「正直に言えば」
settle for ~「~で妥協する」

Take in the Article

A Today's Articleの内容と合うように、空所に適切な日本語を書き入れましょう。

	良い点	悪い点
カスタマーサービス	・仕事内容に (¹.) がある ・有名企業である	(².) ことが苦手
プログラミング	・プログラミングの (³.) がある ・人とあまり話さなくてよいだろう	・(⁴.) が多いかもしれない ・パソコンの前にずっと座っている必要がある

B Today's Articleの内容と合っていればT、そうでなければFを選びましょう。また、問3では、Today's Articleの内容に関するTF問題を英語で作り、ペアで問題を出しあいましょう。

1. The writer is more interested in the programming job than the other job. [T / F]

2. The writer regrets choosing the customer service job. [T / F]

3. _____ [T / F]

C Today's Articleの内容と合うように、次の質問に英語で答えましょう。また、問3では、Today's Articleの内容に関する質問とその答えを英語で作り、ペアで問題を出しあいましょう。

1. Q About how many companies has the writer applied to?

A _____

2. Q Why does the writer think he is not good at talking to people?

A _____

3. Q _____

A _____

Focus on the Signal

自分の言いたいことや主張を少し弱めたり、柔らかく伝えたりしたい場合には、**may** や **might** を用いることができます。日本語では「～だろう」「～かもしれない」に近いニュアンスです。might は may の過去形ですが、過去の意味で用いることは少なく、mayとほとんど同じ意味で用いられます。また、**might want to**「～した方がよい」も、相手への助言を柔らかく伝えたいときによく用いられる表現です。

① She **may [might]** have a cold.
　「彼女は風邪をひいているの**かもしれません**」

② What's that smell? You **might want to** check the oven.
　「これは何の匂いですか。オーブンを確認**した方がよい**ですよ」

また、**probably** は「たぶん」「～だと思う」、**maybe**、**perhaps**、**possibly** は「もしかしたら」「～かもしれない」の意味で用いることができます。probably や possibly は文頭や文中で、maybe や perhaps は文頭に置かれることが多いです。**It is likely that ~.** も同様に、「(たぶん) ～だろう」「～(し) そうだ」などの意味になります。

③ You should **probably** not wear a white suit to the wedding.
　「結婚式には白いスーツを着て行くべきではない**と思います**よ」

④ **It is likely that** the groom will wear a white jacket.
　「**(たぶん)** 新郎は白いジャケットを着る**でしょう**」

Use the Signal

A 空所に入る表現をa～cから選びましょう。文頭に来る語も小文字になっています。

1. He (　　　) already know what it is.
2. (　　　) something is about to change with him.
3. It is (　　　) that the concert will be called off.

a. maybe
b. likely
c. might

B (　　　) 内の語句をヒントにして、次の日本語を英語で表現しましょう。

1. 私たちはこの春、イングランドに行くかもしれません。
(might / England)

＿＿＿＿＿＿＿＿＿＿＿＿＿＿＿＿＿＿＿＿＿＿＿

2. 彼らは正しいのかもしれません。
(likely / right)

＿＿＿＿＿＿＿＿＿＿＿＿＿＿＿＿＿＿＿＿＿＿＿

Opinions on the Article

A ブログに対するレンのコメントに合うように、下の表の空所を埋めましょう。

DL 56　CD 56

 Ren I recommend the customer service job because you should get a job that you are interested in. Once you get a job, it will become a big part of your life. If the job is interesting, you can work more enthusiastically. On the other hand, if the job is boring, you might lose your passion for work. If you really like your job, you can overcome any difficulties.

就くべき職	(¹.) の仕事
理由	興味がある仕事に就くべき ・仕事が興味深ければ、より (². 　　　　　) 働くことができる ・仕事が退屈だと、仕事に対する (³. 　　　) を失うかもしれない ・本当に好きな仕事であれば、苦手なことも (⁴. 　　) できる

B 表の内容と合うように、ブログに対するリズのコメントの空所に入る語を選択肢から選びましょう。

DL 57　CD 57

就くべき職	プログラミングの仕事
理由	得意な仕事に就くべき ・経験があることは有利 ・会社をリードする存在になり，同僚より多くお金を稼げるかもしれない ・きつくて退屈な仕事とよく言われるが、進んだ知識や才能があれば楽しいだろう

 Liz I recommend the (¹. 　　　　　　　　) job because you should get a job that you are good at. Your programming experience will surely be an (². 　　　　　　　　). You may even become a leader at your company and (³. 　　　　　　　) more money than your colleagues someday. It is often said that a programming job is tough and boring, but you will probably enjoy it with your advanced knowledge and (⁴. 　　　　　　　)!

advantage　　earn　　programming　　talent

Express Your Opinions

どちらの仕事に就くべきかについて、ブログへのコメントを書きましょう。

A 前ページの表にならい、意見をまとめましょう。

就くべき職	
理由	

B 前ページのコメントにならい、上の表にまとめた内容を英語で書きましょう。

I recommend the (   ) job because
(   ).

_____

_____

_____

_____

_____

☑ 使用した表現があればチェックをし、これまでのUnitで学んだ表現を使った場合は最後の□の横に書きましょう。

☐ may   ☐ perhaps
☐ might   ☐ possibly
☐ might want to   ☐ It is likely that ~.
☐ probably   ☐
☐ maybe

C ペアやグループで発表しましょう。

UNIT 15

Students do more than just study.

あなたのガクチカは？

自分の言いたいことをまとめる表現　[in other words]

Important Expressions

🎧 DL 58　💿 CD 58

[　　]内のアルファベットを並び替えて、下線部の日本語を表す英単語を完成させましょう。

1. 私は高校生活をトランペット<u>に捧げ</u>ました。　　　[a c d e e i t] (d _ _ _ _ _ _ _)

2. いろいろな人と<u>つながる</u>ことは大切です。　　　[c e n n o t] (c _ _ _ _ _ _)

3. 私は昨年、文化祭<u>を運営し</u>ました。　　　[a e g i n r z] (o _ _ _ _ _ _ _)

4. 私はそのレースで<u>1位</u>を取りました。　　　[a c e l] (p _ _ _ _)

5. ペット<u>を引き取っ</u>て世話をするのは難しいです。　　　[d t p o] (a _ _ _ _)

Signal Check

　　で囲まれている日本語に対応する英語に○をつけましょう。

1. Japanese has *hiragana*, *katakana*, and *kanji*. In other words, you must learn many characters.

日本語にはひらがなもカタカナも漢字もあります。　言い換えると、あなたはたくさんの文字を学ばなければなりません。

2. Her stories are simple and witty. In brief, she is a great storyteller.

彼女の話は簡潔で機知に富んでいます。　まとめると、彼女は話が上手いのです。

3. I think it is effective. To put it another way, I don't think there is a more effective option.

それは有効だと思います。　言い換えると、それ以上有効な選択肢はないと思います。

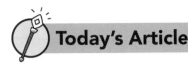
🎧 DL 59 　 💿 CD 59

次の求人への応募を読みましょう。

自分の言いたいことをまとめる表現に注意して読もう！

Tell us about your extracurricular activities in university.

In university, I dedicated my extra time to two main extracurricular activities. First, I was a member of the English-Speaking Society (ESS). It is a club for people who want to improve their English and connect with foreign people. We did a variety of volunteer activities. For example, we assisted new international students. In other words, we volunteered to help them with whatever they needed. We also organized English speech contests together with ESS students in other universities. In my second year, I got first place with a speech about culture shock. In my third year, I was put in charge of communication between the participating universities. In brief, I would say that the ESS taught me a lot about communication and organization.

I also volunteered at a nearby dog shelter. I learned that many shelters are flooded with abandoned dogs but don't have enough staff to care for all of them. To put it another way, many dogs have to be put down because the shelters cannot care for them all. I wanted to help, so I volunteered every Sunday at the shelter. I helped walk the dogs, feed them, and sometimes helped with cleaning, too. The most important thing was finding people to adopt the dogs, so I helped organize a visit from our local TV station. With their help, adoptions increased, and many dogs were saved. In conclusion, I was happy that I could use my extra time in university to help others, and I hope I can do more after I graduate.

Proceed ⟩

Notes

extracurricular activity「学外活動」　be put in charge of ~「~を任される」
be flooded with ~「~で溢れかえる」　abandoned dog「捨てられた犬」　be put down「殺処分される」

Take in the Article

A Today's Articleの内容と合うように、空所に適切な日本語を書き入れましょう。

	活動内容	達成したこと
ESS	・新しい (**1.** 　　　　　　　) の手助け ・他大学のESSの学生と英語スピーチコンテストを運営	スピーチコンテストで (**2.** 　　) した
ドッグシェルター	・犬の散歩や餌やり、掃除の手伝い ・地元の (**3.** 　　　　　　　) の取材を手配	(**4.** 　　　　　　　) が増え、多くの犬が救われた

B Today's Articleの内容と合っていればT、そうでなければFを選びましょう。また、問3では、Today's Articleの内容に関するTF問題を英語で作り、ペアで問題を出しあいましょう。

1. The writer spoke about dog shelters in the speech contest. 　　　　　　[T / F]

2. Many dog shelters don't have enough staff members to take care of the dogs. 　[T / F]

3. _____ [T / F]

C Today's Articleの内容と合うように、次の質問に英語で答えましょう。また、問3では、Today's Articleの内容に関する質問とその答えを英語で作り、ペアで問題を出しあいましょう。

1. **Q** According to the writer, what did the ESS teach her?

A _____

2. **Q** When did the writer volunteer at the dog shelter?

A _____

3. **Q** _____

A _____

Focus on the Signal

自分の言いたいことをまとめる場合には、**in other words** を用いることができます。日本語の「**言い換えると**」に近い意味で、それまでに述べてきた内容を1文程度で簡潔にまとめる場合によく用いられます。

① I think his work is brilliant. **In other words**, I want to work with him more.

「彼の仕事ぶりは素晴らしいと思います。**言い換えると**、私は彼ともっと仕事がしたいです」

似たような表現に、**that is (to say)**、**to put it another way**、**in brief**、**in short**、**in conclusion**、**to sum up** などがあります。「つまり」「要するに」「まとめると」などの日本語に対応します。いずれも文頭で用いることが多い表現です。文と文をつなげることはできないので、注意しましょう。

② Your report has too many mistakes. **That is to say**, I can't accept it.

「君のレポートは間違いが多すぎます。**つまり**、私はそれを受理できません」

③ I like his eyes, ears, and the way he barks. **In conclusion**, I love my dog.

「彼の目も、耳も、そして鳴き方も好きです。**まとめると**、私は自分の犬が大好きです」

Use the Signal

A 空所に入る表現をa〜cから選びましょう。

1. Classical music is said to be good for pregnant women. In other words, (   ).

2. We need a lot of wine for the party. To put it another way, (   ).

3. Most of us don't know how to use this new machine well. In brief, (   ).

a. we need a lot of money

b. it's good for unborn babies

c. it won't be so helpful

B (   ) 内の語句をヒントにして、次の日本語を英語で表現しましょう。

1. 結論を言うと、私は彼の意見に賛成です。

(conclusion)

_____

2. 言い換えると、平和とは待つものではなく、達成するものです。

(something / wait for / achieve)

_____

Opinions on the Article

A 大学での課外活動についてトムが求人への応募に書いた内容に合うように、下の表の空所を埋めましょう。　🎧 DL 60　💿 CD 60

Tom

In university, I am mainly dedicating my extra time to my part-time job. I am working as a cram school teacher. From my teaching experience, I have learned that teaching is more than just having knowledge. It was sometimes difficult for me to explain even very simple ideas to children. In other words, teaching children is different from teaching adults.

課外活動	(¹.　　　　　　) のアルバイト
具体的なエピソード	(².　　　　) を持っているだけでは教えることはできないということを学んだ。非常に単純な (³.　　　　) でさえも子どもに教えるのは難しいことがあった。言い換えると、子どもに教えることは大人に教えることと (⁴.　　　　)

B 表の内容と合うように、大学での課外活動についてミオが求人への応募に書いた内容の空所に入る語を選択肢から選びましょう。　🎧 DL 61　💿 CD 61

課外活動	部活動
具体的なエピソード	大学のブラスバンドのメンバーで、大学2年生のとき演奏会の企画・運営を担当した。多くの困難に直面したが、演奏会をなんとか成功裏に終えることができたときに達成感を感じた。要するに、私は部活動でイベントを企画・実行することの難しさと楽しさを学んだ

Mio

In university, I am mainly dedicating my extra time to club activities. I am a member of the brass band at university. When I was a (¹.　　　　　　), I was in (².　　　　　　) of organizing our concerts. We faced a lot of difficulties, but we (³.　　　　　　) to have successful concerts. I really felt a sense of accomplishment then. In brief, I learned the difficulty and (⁴.　　　　　) of planning and hosting events through club activities.

charge　joy　managed　sophomore

Express Your Opinions

大学での課外活動について，あなた自身の経験を書きましょう。

A 前ページの表にならい、経験をまとめましょう。

課外活動	
具体的なエピソード	

B 前ページの求人への応募にならい、上の表にまとめた内容を英語で書きましょう。

In university, I am mainly dedicating my extra time to (

).＿＿＿＿＿＿＿＿＿＿＿＿＿＿

＿＿＿＿＿＿＿＿＿＿＿＿＿＿＿＿＿＿＿＿＿＿＿＿＿＿＿＿＿＿

＿＿＿＿＿＿＿＿＿＿＿＿＿＿＿＿＿＿＿＿＿＿＿＿＿＿＿＿＿＿

＿＿＿＿＿＿＿＿＿＿＿＿＿＿＿＿＿＿＿＿＿＿＿＿＿＿＿＿＿＿

＿＿＿＿＿＿＿＿＿＿＿＿＿＿＿＿＿＿＿＿＿＿＿＿＿＿＿＿＿＿

＿＿＿＿＿＿＿＿＿＿＿＿＿＿＿＿＿＿＿＿＿＿＿＿＿＿＿＿＿＿

☑ 使用した表現があればチェックをし、これまでのUnitで学んだ表現を使った場合は最後の□の横に書きましょう。

☐ in other words   ☐ in short

☐ that is (to say)   ☐ in conclusion

☐ to put it another way   ☐ to sum up

☐ in brief   ☐

C ペアやグループで発表しましょう。

memo

本書にはCD（別売）があります

Get the Signal!
Discourse Markers for Reading and Writing
リーディング&ライティングの「目」じるし

2023年1月20日　初版第1刷発行
2023年2月20日　初版第2刷発行

著者　　佐　藤　　　選
　　　　内　野　駿　介
　　　　Ayed Hasian

発行者　　福　岡　正　人
発行所　　株式会社　金星堂
（〒101-0051）　東京都千代田区神田神保町 3-21
Tel　（03）3263-3828（営業部）
　　　（03）3263-3997（編集部）
Fax　（03）3263-0716
https://www.kinsei-do.co.jp

編集担当　池田恭子・四條雪菜　　　　　　　　　Printed in Japan
印刷所・製本所／三美印刷株式会社

ISBN978-4-7647-4181-2　C1082